$\mathcal{P}$raise for *An American Story*

We met Gary Buehler for the first time three years ago on a snowy night in December. Joan Pedzich – the peerless leader of our small writing group – introduced him as an old friend who was writing a memoir. He was tanned and healthy looking with perfect manners, a gentleman in every sense of the word. He called Joan "Joanie" and it was obvious that she loved it.

At our meetings, we would read aloud the pages we had written since our last encounter. Joan always had a poem or a short story written in the most exquisite prose. Melanie brought poetry and short stories from the real world of her busy life. Rae-Ellen always read a new chapter from her novel. But Gary – Gary brought something entirely new – an authentic voice telling stories about his life growing up in a small town in upstate New York. That very first meeting, he told us about when he had polio and we say "told" because that is the power of his writing: the characters – the action – the story – just leap off the pages. This book is a collection of those stories which in the most understated way illuminate a way of life. Gary always said the book was only written for his family – but his powerful language and strong sense of humanity make this a story for everyone.

Joan died completely unexpectedly just over a year ago. It was the three of us who came up with the title for Gary's book – and we are so sorry that Joanie is not here for the publication of *An American Story*. She was the first reader to appreciate the way Gary's straightforward style allowed us to become completely immersed in the landscape of another time and we know her support meant a great deal. It was truly an honor for our whole group to be part of the writing of this wonderful book.

An American Story will warm your heart – it is a trip back to a time when winters were colder and having fun required imagination and ingenuity. With candor and love, Gary Buehler takes us from his early days as a young boy through his coming of age and fulfilling career to his current life, rich with family. Prepare for a beautiful journey filled with trials and victories, challenges and revelations, but most of all, the enduring spirit of the American Dream.

Rae-Ellen Kavey
Melanie Krebs

AN AMERICAN STORY

AN AMERICAN STORY

Gary J. Buehler

An American Story

Copyright © 2018

by Gary J. Buehler

cover design by Lucy Swerdfeger

Published by

New Education Press

NewEducationPress.com

ISBN:

978-1-932842-87-6 — $ 14.95

Printed in the United States of America

Dedicated to

The love of my life, Charlotte
and our children
Tonja, Tammy, and Todd
and their children
Kyle, Daniel, Hanna and Gavin

With special thanks to

Members of my writing group

Joani, Rae-Ellen, and Melanie

Advisors, Reviewers and Editors

William "Bill" Morris and Steven Swerdfeger, Ph.D.

Family Tree

Very incomplete but all you need to know for these stories

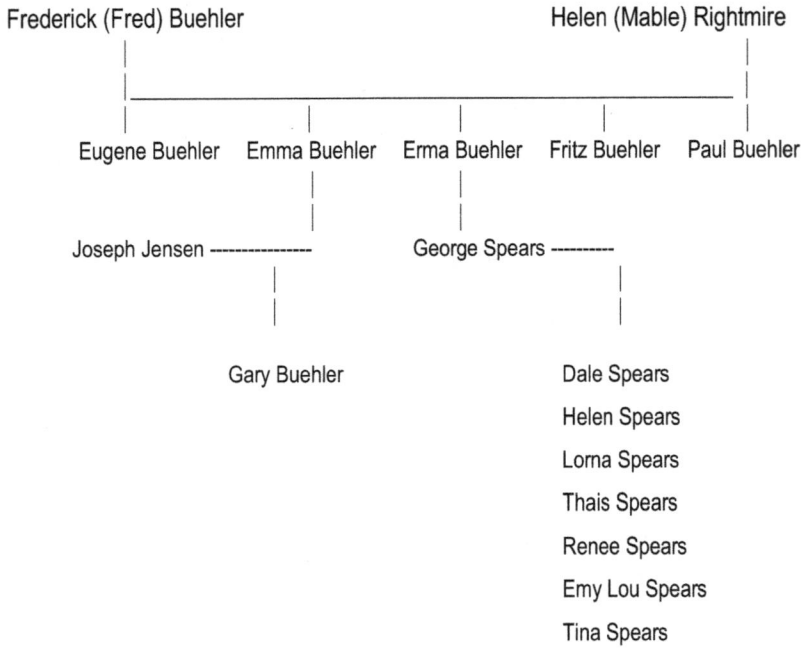

Frederick (Fred) Buehler   Helen (Mable) Rightmire

Eugene Buehler   Emma Buehler   Erma Buehler   Fritz Buehler   Paul Buehler

Joseph Jensen ----------------   George Spears ----------

Gary Buehler   Dale Spears

Helen Spears

Lorna Spears

Thais Spears

Renee Spears

Emy Lou Spears

Tina Spears

CONTENTS

Prologue

The "why" of this compilation of stories is the direct consequence of our oldest daughter Tonja saying, "Dad, you need to write these stories down." I have told them repeatedly at holiday and family gatherings and celebrations over countless years. For a few Christmases, one of Tonja's presents was always a book on the theme of "How to write your life story." I finally took the not so subtle hint seriously, conceded, and began to write. That was a few years ago. I then realized I really wanted to record these stories not just for our children but for our grandchildren, perhaps other family members who may be interested, and for future generations.

My first effort consisting of some 100 pages or so can be found stuffed in the back of one of my file cabinet drawers. I had it edited by a professional and a good friend and with his advice and feedback he provided along with the editing, I thought it best to start over. This process did not result in a loss of a friend but I did have to pick up the tab twice at a Starbucks for our meetings. What motivated me to try again was that there was one story of my first car in that draft effort that I sent it to three car-themed national magazines. To my surprise and delight, all three published it. And yes, it is included in this draft also. I'll soon find out what you think and you don't even have to spend $5.95 to buy the magazine.

Then I decided to get serious about putting a few of these stories down on paper. I thought I would attend a writer's workshop and discussed this with my good friend Joani Pedzich. Bob (her husband) and Charlotte and I have been friends for almost fifty years. Bob and I taught together as newly hired teachers and over the years we have vacationed together. Joani was a published author and had been writing creatively as well as professionally all her life, was trained as a librarian, and attended many writing retreats and workshops over the years. She told me she would inquire around to try to find a good "fit" for me and provide a recommendation for a workshop that I might consider attending. I was astonished when she called back in a few days to ask me if I would mind joining her own writing group and if I minded that there three women in it. In almost the same breath, she mentioned that she had already spoken with the two other members of her group and they were OK with the idea. A couple of years have passed and now I find myself writing this Prologue for you.

The stories that follow are memories of childhood, coming of age, and life so far as I have lived it. As I share these with you I am reminded of the words of Marcus J Borg, Ph.D., who was an American New Testament scholar, theologian and author whom I admired. In a lecture that Charlotte and I attended a number of years ago, I remember one of his opening lines, "Now I don't know if it happened this way or not, but I know these stories to be true." This may be something to think about as you work your way through the chapters that follow.

I began to write a memoir but it turned out to be a faux one, that is, it tells some of the events in my life but it is not sequential. As you shall see, my family or, better stated, my extended family was not at all evident to me in the beginning as a young child growing up. It was a puzzle for me to figure out and put together and try to make some sense out of it. To complicate things just a bit, I didn't have the cover of the puzzle box with the picture on it, just the pieces in the box. So as you are about to discover, I started with the straight edges of the puzzle, building the border all the way around, and finally the family picture emerges. I trust that my approach provides insights to the significant events, places, and people in my life as a pre-teen and as a teenager. At least that's my hope for you, the reader. They may be some adult musing also for a smile or two.

So grab hold, hang on tight, buckle your seat belt and come along on the ride with me.

The World without Color

Although I never met my father, a photograph of him in his Navy uniform sits on my dresser in our bedroom. In May of 1945, WWII was winding down and in its last days in Europe with the advancement of allied forces into Berlin and Hitler's bunker. My father, mother's brothers and her older cousins, were in the Army, Navy or Air Force. This particular day in May was my first venture out of my confined world in more than seven months. I remember begging Aunt Erma who was driving with grandma in the front seat to go slower. "Please, please slow down." We were on a two lane highway and holding up traffic driving very slowly. I was in the back seat of the 1937 Chevy looking out the windows trying to see both sides of the road at once while at the same time straining to see out of the windshield so that I would be certain to not miss a thing. The blue water of the lake was a wonderful contrast to the vibrant greens of the lawns, shrubbery, and conifer trees. The giant oaks provided yet another distinct and different shade of green. Car horns were blaring behind us as we pulled over to the side of the road. I begged to just stay where we were as I had never seen so many rich and detailed colors in such a long time. What I remember most of the past year were trees without leaves and white snow covering everything as I looked from my bed beyond the windows of the sanitary brick building that was my world and home. I was now free of that detention and on my way to my grandmother's house in this fascinating Technicolor world.

I was just 4 years old and for many months prior to this everything seemed to be in monochrome. The woman with that little hat on her head was dressed in all white. Even her shoes were white. The man's lab coat was also white as were his shoes. The room was illuminated by brilliant white lights and a huge one hung from a movable fixture on the ceiling above my bed.

Just a week before, I was home with my grandmother and remember being very ill. I was hot and nauseated for several days. The doctor made a home visit and his diagnoses was that I had the "grippe." The doctor left enough sulfa tablets for ten days for grandma to give to me. Five days passed and my temperature returned to normal. I remember being carried from the bedroom to the living room sofa. As I struggled to get up I was unable straighten my legs or even extend them to the floor. I was like a newborn. My knees were flexed up against my abdomen, my neck was stiff and sore, and I was having spasms in both legs. I remember being bundled up in blankets and taken to Strong Memorial Hospital. I came down with "grippe" (influenza) on October 2nd and on the 11th I was in a bed in the emergency room. The woman and man dressed in white turned me over on my side and I noticed out of the corner of my eye a big shiny chrome needle. As I was being held by the nurse and my grandmother so that I wouldn't move, I felt a sharp sting in my lower back and the man said something about spinal fluid and that he was going to have it sent to the lab. I was examined by the doctor and I was still having spasms in the hamstrings of both legs. When the doctor asked me to sit up in the bed I couldn't. Now it was a waiting game for the lab results.

I spent the next 15 days in a hospital room and I learned that the man in the white lab coat who came to see me every day was Dr. Schwartz. He told my grandmother and mother that he first thought I had poliomyelitis but was not sure which one of the three types. He explained that Type I results in paralysis of limbs while Type II leads to asymptomatic cases but still can paralyze or lead to death and Type III was the rarest of the three but attacks the lower portion of the brain leading to paralysis of the diaphragm and being unable to breathe on your own. He further explained that after the lab work had been completed it was determined that I had Type II acute anterior poliomyelitis and the good news was that it was a non-paralytic strain. The doctor's instructions for my hospital stay indicated that "…hot packs are to be applied to both legs and massages to all muscles affected." Dr Swartz's final prescription was written on October 27, 1944. I was four years and two months old. I was to be transferred and assigned to the Children's Convalescent Hospital for a period of six months. The diagnosis simply read; "Poliomyelitis patient under the long-term care of Dr. Schwartz with continued recumbency on a firm mattress, daily hot baths and packs until soreness and stiffness are eliminated with massages and muscular exercises to all muscles affected."

These dates, descriptions, procedures and prescriptions were detailed and recorded in my patient folders at Strong Memorial Hospital and obtained recently through the Freedom of Information Law (FOIL).

This diagnosis translated into practice, for me as a 4 year old, of a daily routine of a breakfast tray delivered to my bed, an offer of a bed pan and a mid-morning juice drink which we were allowed to decide on, my favorite being grape. Every morning a washing machine on wheels was rolled into the ward, filled with very hot water. The nurse would then soak the towels and run them through the ringer and immediately wrap them around my legs. They made my legs feel like they were on fire because they were so hot. She would then move on to the next bed and then on to all the beds in the ward. Circling back to where she had started, the towels had cooled and were removed. Then the leg muscles were massaged followed by several minutes of leg exercises. After the lunch tray was served we were transferred in wheelchairs to the bath tanks. This area contained large stainless steel vats with hot water circulating in them. We were lifted out of our chairs, placed on a lift which was a frame with canvas stretched on it and it was then lowered into the tank. After being in the tank for a long period of time, we were lifted and our affected limbs were hand massaged. We were then taken back to our bed for more exercise on the polio affected parts of our bodies. The dinner tray was always a treat as we had some type of dessert. Before bed time another juice delivery was made and once again we usually had a choice of which type we wanted. Lights out meant no talking and total silence was expected by the nurses. We could always tell when a new child arrived due to the crying and sobbing at bed time and throughout the night. As I recall, I acted the same way my first day so I felt empathy for the new arrivals. The night nurse could not comfort you as your mother could. Lights out — no talking was not always a quiet time. Night time was a time for crying, feeling sad, loneliness and a longing for your mother and home.

The concept of time for a 4 year old is more of an abstraction than anything real. Time really had little meaning other than what was happening at the moment. I'm not sure how much time passed, nor am I sure whose idea it was, but there we were, three little four and five year olds lined up in our wheelchairs. Then on the count of three we were off racing down the long hallway toward the closed fire doors. I was pushing with my arms as fast as I could when I reached the first set of doors and I was going way too fast to stop.

The extended legs of the wooden wheelchair hit the glass panels of the door. Even with the wire embedded into the safety glass, the panels cracked into spider web like splinters. The race was over, I had won! The sound of the breaking glass brought the floor nurse running. The three of us took a highly excited tongue lashing and when we were asked who was responsible for the carnage; two little fingers from the other boys were pointed in my direction. Perhaps as punishment, I really do not know, the nurse pushed me down the hallway to the last set of fire doors at the other end of the hall and into yet another long corridor eventually leading to the laundry storage room. Huge bags of bed linens and towels were stacked on all three sides leaving just room enough for my wheelchair so the door could be closed. There was one light fixture hanging from ceiling that provided illumination and once again I found myself in a world of white. Large laundry bags seemed to fill the tiny room. It was a time without ending before the nurse returned and pushed me back to the ward and placed me in my bed. Even at four years old I knew it would be several days before my grandmother and my mother would come for a visit and I knew I had to wait to tell them what had happened. Sunday was a very important day for the entire ward since only immediate family members could visit the hospital. Visitation was allowed once during the week and I knew that this was always on Sunday.

At the Children's Convalescent Hospital my colorless world was constant. The nurses' white uniforms were crisp and starched complete with white shoes and the ever present little white nurse's hat bobby-pinned to their hair. The doctors' lab coats and orderlies' uniforms were white along with everyone's shoes. All the bedsteads were white enameled steel with white sheets and pillows. In our ward there were two huge bulky white cylinder machines that enveloped a child with only his or her head appearing out one end. These were interesting but scary pieces of apparatus as they were always running and making noise. All of us kids in the ward could see these machines from our beds but we were not allowed to go near them when we were in our wheelchairs. My grandmother told me this piece of equipment was called an iron lung. I wanted to know why the children were never allowed out of the machine and put in their own wheelchair to be taken with the rest of us to the rooftop patio and wrapped in thick wool blankets and allowed to sit in the sun. Grandma said that the children in the iron lung could not leave because they would not be able to breathe on their own and would die. It was then that I realized how exceedingly fortunate I was.

One spring day there was a huge thunderstorm and the lights went out and the result was a flurry of activity. Nurses, doctors, and orderlies were running to the machines and attaching long handles. All of us watched as the handles were being pushed and pulled back and forth. We had no clue what was happening but we found this change of pace and the hustle and bustle of this new activity to be somewhat entertaining. Actually we could sense a great deal of tension in the air. Obviously as a four-year-old I really did not have an understanding of the implications of the impact of the thunderstorm. It was simply a nice break in the day-to-day routine.

Parents and family were only allowed to visit once a week on Sunday after 12:00 noon. I fondly remember one family visitation day in particular. I was given a bag of 50 wonderfully colored glass marbles to play with that provided several days of entertainment for me and many others in our ward. That bag of marbles was like holding a rainbow in your hands. Each one was a different design and color from greens to blues and yellow to orange with wavy colored bands inside each one.

What a pleasant contrast these bright colored glass balls were to the colorless and bleak ward and the white uniforms and background. That evening, after all the visitors had left, I had my bag of marbles and I began playing with them on the bed. I put a couple of them in my mouth and felt them with my tongue and they were so smooth that I put a few more in and soon my mouth was filled with saliva and accidently one slipped down my throat. It went down so easy that I almost didn't feel it. I added a few more marbles to replace the lost one and then I tried to see how many marbles I could actually put in my mouth. It wasn't long after that unintentionally another one or two slipped down my throat. That didn't seem to hurt so I tried to see how many I could swallow. To my surprise, 50 wasn't even the slightest challenge. When the nurse came on her final round before "lights out" she found the empty bag on my bed. She wanted to know where my marbles were. I wasn't about to tell her what happened so I told her that they had rolled off my bed. She was down on her hands and knees looking around for them and soon after another nurse joined in trying to find the missing marbles. When I was confronted by both nurses wanting to know what I had done with the marbles, I had to admit that I swallowed all of them. The doctor was called and I was examined and then there was a long discussion with the nurses in the hallway. I was treated to a special glass of my favorite grape juice that evening before bed time. As the night wore on I realized that my tummy felt a little funny but I was in for a huge surprise the first thing in the morning. I was put on a potty chair right next to the desk at the nurses' station where I spent most of the day. Everyone but the nurses enjoyed the rat-a-tat-tat sound of the marbles hitting the stainless steel pan attached to the potty chair. Apparently all 50 marbles had to be accounted for so I had the opportunity to sit on the potty chair the following day. At some point in time somehow the nurses and the doctor figured out that all the marbles had been reclaimed and I had no idea how they came to this conclusion. I was just very happy that I didn't have to spend any more time next to the nurses's desk. I asked for my marbles back. I didn't get them. All I wanted were the marbles because of their wonderful colors. They added so much to my otherwise colorless world.

Now I was again in a brightly colored world in the car after being discharged. Horns finally stopped blaring and all the cars had driven by us and the old brown 1937 Chevy was slowly moving down the road again. A half of a year is an eternity for a little guy but my world of white was now in Technicolor once more and all of this before my 5th birthday! And the best part of all was that I wasn't going home in a wheelchair! I was going to be carried! No wheel chair, crutches, metal leg braces to travel home with me, just a limp, exercises to do, follow-up doctor appointments, and in my future, an experimental operation and many months spent in a body cast every night. The operation was a success when it was completed 2 years later in 1947!

1519

I remember every detail as if it happened yesterday. Returning home in the car from the Children's Convalescent Hospital, I was still begging Aunt Erma to drive as slowly as possible. I just wanted to bask in the beautiful world of color all around me. The '37 Chevy gradually made its way up the raise on Emerson Street past the swampy bog and the pond at the foot of the hill before coming to the driveway of Gram's house at 1519 Emerson Street. If you were to search for this address today within the City of Rochester you will only find a vast industrial complex where my grandparents' home once stood.

The Chevy chugged passed the four rock piles in the front lawn along the side of the street that were framed by the same number of flowering bushes bordering the cinder, dirt, and mud driveway. It was nearly a half a year earlier when I was taken to the hospital from here and now I was very excited to be returning to what I knew as my home. Aunt Erma pulled the car up in front of the pair of side hinged front doors of the aged and weathered single car garage. The sedan stopped right in front of the steps leading up to the back porch and then to the door of the kitchen. Erma turned the ignition key to the off position and I was carried up the porch stairs, through the kitchen and into the living room and gently placed on the sofa.

It was from this very garage roof just a few years later where I made my first umbrella parachute jump pretending that I was a WWII US Air Force Paratrooper being dropped behind enemy lines. The rest of the paratroopers that were on the roof with me declined to jump from the imaginary B-17 when I hurt my ankle on a rough landing in the driveway and limped away. The garage was also the perfect place to

10

spend my time when it was raining. It was the best place to fix the flat tire on 'brother' Paul's hand-me-down old front-end sprung Schwinn bike as well as assorted other projects like building the Pirate's treasure chest out of a salted cod fish box to later be buried in the field behind the garage for the treasure chest hunt. My fabricated map was covered with candle wax and burned around the edges to give it the proper antique patina. Other rainy day events that took place here were the many "crash and burn" automobile 'accidents' caused by a book of matches, lighter fluid, and plastic cars.

My parents were Helen (Mable) and Fredrick (Fred) John or Franklin Buehler (Buchler). Fred was born on November 4, 1882. His birth record lists John as his middle name while his marriage license indicates that it is Franklin. Mable Helen Rightmire was born on November 25, 1895. They were married on October 15, 1913 and had six children; the first born was Eugene in 1914, followed by Emma 1916, then Erma in 1919, Fredrick (Fritz) in 1923, Paul was born 1932 and finally me, and I was born in 1940. I know the dates, years, and math do not add up nor make sense, but don't get too far ahead of my story...

Grams and Gramp's house, although within the city limits, did not have an indoor bathroom. Personal needs were taken care of by a small one-hole privy built onto the back of the garage which was reached by a foot path leading from the back porch. Numerous times, many late night or early morning quick trips to the privy were made bare-footed on the frosted ground when time did not permit or it didn't seem important to bother putting on a pair of shoes or boots. In the summer, the path to the privy was always lined with colorful tall Holly Hocks growing by the garage. The floor plan of the house was reminiscent of the shotgun houses of the Deep South — that is, three rooms in a line from front to back, narrow and long. The house had a front door but it was never used as this room facing the street served as the one and only bedroom. The middle room was the living room and the back room, the kitchen. The three rooms were very small and the house was 650 sq. ft. total. The tiny porch off the kitchen also contained the stairs to the cellar. The house was not exactly what you would call roomy, but before I joined the family, it served as a home for seven people! Paul was the only one of

Gram's and Gramp's five birth children still at home when I arrived on the scene. 'Brother Paul was eight years older than me. Paul's other four siblings were older and no longer living at home at that time.

As a child growing up in this house, the front bedroom had Gram's and Gramp's double bed on one side, a built-in closet on the wall at the foot of the bed with just enough space to walk between the bedstead and the closet with the sliding cloth curtain. The front door of the house had a dresser placed in front of it with a wash basin and mirror sitting on it. This is where Gramps shaved every morning using a straight razor and the leather sharpening strap was attached to the bed post. There was a window behind the head board. Next to the dresser, the foot of the bunk bed was against the front wall and was placed along the side wall. At the head of the bunk bed there was just enough room to walk between it and two dressers along the interior wall of the room. One of these dressers was Gramp's and Paul and I shared the other one next to it. Gram's dresser was the one that sat in front of the front door of the house. I was not allowed to go in other dresser draws. I couldn't resist temptation and when I was all alone in the house and I would go through Gramp's dresser drawers and Paul's as they were always a treasure trove of delights for explorations for me. Gramp's treasures in his dresser included a box of straight razors, a railroad pocket watch with chain, folding paper money under the box of razors, a gold wrist watch, a five dollar gold piece, silver dollar certificates, stock and bond certificates, coins and his clothes. Paul's drawers held Boy Scout goodies including a pocket knife, hatchet, canteen and always some loose change and not much else other than his clothes except for some pictures of his girl friend Lorraine.

The flowered wall-papered bedroom was separated from the middle living room by a set of solid wood style French doors of which only one was used as the maple sofa was placed in front of the other door. A coffee table and two matching maple chairs completed the living room furniture. In the other corner of the room was Gramp's reading chair, floor lamp and a floor model cabinet radio. Six years later Gram's and Gramp's first television set would be placed on an end table by the sofa. After school TV programs were the Kate Smith Hour and the Mickey Mouse Club on the rare days when I didn't want to play outside on my own until I was called home for dinner. Between the living room and the kitchen was a door way. The door was always left open into the living room because behind the door was a steel wardrobe used for winter clothing, fishing poles, tackle box, and guns for hunting. We never had a phone but in 1951 we did have a new TV! Rare emergency phone calls were made and received at the Potts' residence who were our neighbors across the street. A phone call was a major event of stress, pressure, and running as fast as you could because they were expensive for each minute of usage. When the new TV arrived the radio evening programs we listened to gave way to Gramp's favorite Friday night's boxing events always on at 10:00 pm and way past my bedtime but I could listen to them in bed from the front room.

The back wall of the third room which was the kitchen had a single built-in cot next to the gas cook stove. The wall near the stove had a Hosier cabinet and next to it was a counter and cabinets which ran L-shaped along a part of the adjacent wall. More cabinets and the kitchen sink ended at the chimney that came up from the basement which was next to the doorway leading into the living room. The wall along the driveway had room for the ice box which later was replaced by a new refrigerator a year after the war ended. As a little kid, I remember the ice man delivering blocks of ice every Saturday morning. Next to the ice box sat one of the extra chairs from the kitchen table set. When I was old enough to go to Kindergarten Paul and I had our breakfasts together and made our lunches at the table before walking to school. Breakfast was usually a half of loaf of bread toasted in the oven under the broiler. The several pieces of toast were either torn into small bits in a bowl and covered with milk and sugar or covered with homemade canned jam or jelly. Breakfast was a great start to the day even though Paul insisted I chew each piece of toast 25 times before swallowing and with my mouth closed. Later in my grammar and middle school years the wooden table was used as a desk for home work.

The house was heated by a coal furnace located in the center of the basement. On the rear wall of the cellar was a wooden coal bin. Next to that half of the basement was a small sink which drained into a sump, a wringer washing machine, and a mangle. There was a gas heater and a tank for hot water but it was not an on-demand automatic affair. In order to have water for taking baths, washing clothes, or for any other reason you had to plan ahead a minimum of at least an hour. The heater was a 2 foot high by 8 inch circular coiled tube within a steel cylinder with a small door and a gas burner at the bottom which had to be lit by a match. The heater was attached to a steel upright water tank and as the water was heated in the coils it flowed up into the tank. You could tell how much hot water you had by running your hand from the bottom to the top of the tank until you felt warmth. When water was needed on Mondays for laundry or Wednesdays and Saturdays for baths, my chore was to run down stairs and light the gas burner and then run back and forth every 15 minutes or so to let folks know when the tank was fully heated. Baths were taken in a round wash tub in the basement which was placed on the floor when needed and were taken in order from the youngest to the oldest. Other days of the week, sponge baths were part of the daily routine each morning utilizing the kitchen sink along with brushing your teeth and combing your hair. Bed time teeth brushing and washing also took place at the kitchen sink.

The mysterious and magical wonders of the cellar were always a delight for me. I loved that Gram sent me down each evening to pick a dessert for the dinner meal from her canned goods that filled the many shelves along the walls. Choices varied from peaches, pears, cherries, plums to jams and jellies of every imaginable fruit, color, and variety. There were even quarts of canned white and red grape juice. One of my favorite Sunday night light dinners before going to church was Gram's tomato juice on elbow macaroni with a pad of make believe butter and some small chunks of Velveeta cheese on top. Since I was alone in the house every day after school until folks came home from work well after 5 PM, my afternoon treat was to take a potato or two and place them on the inside shelf around the coal fire in the furnace. After 45 minutes of baking I could retrieve the potatoes, cut them in half, put pads of margarine on them along with salt and pepper and have a great afternoon snack. One time I was playing with my neighborhood buddies and told them about this little snack trick of mine and asked them if they wanted to try it. Of course they did! Gram bought potatoes by the 50 pound bag but margarine was purchased one plastic squeeze bag at a time. My adventures in the basement came to an end not because the potatoes disappeared too soon but because the margarine did! A new ruling for after school activities was quickly established and the cellar was placed off limits.

Thus my young years at 1519 Emerson Street are mostly remembered as happy times growing up and this was our home until I was 14 when we moved into a newly built home in the suburbs in Greece at 55 Laura Drive. Although they were fun years on Emerson Street, my life took many twists and turns and I garnered new insights into life as we shall see ...

Brothers, Sisters, Uncles and Aunts
Which Make No Sense at All ... Until

I don't know any of the specific details, but my mother, Emma, at age 23, met a young man who was in the Navy and was from the Rochester area. His name was Joseph Jensen and they dated for a period of time. I have two pictures of him on my dresser, one in his Navy uniform and the other is a Gannet Company photograph which shows him posed with his camera as a *Democrat & Chronicle* newspaper staff photographer. I never met him in person but, later in my life, when I was in my fifties, I decided to search for him. It turned out to be a simple task. I asked my mother for his name which I did not know and she shared that with me and a few other significant details. I found his name in the local phone directory and called the number. His wife answered. I introduced myself and explained who I was and why I was calling.

I discovered that he, his wife, and family had lived within five miles of where I grew up as a teenager in the Town of Greece. We set a time to get together and she was most willing and invited me to meet at her home. Her husband had told her before they were married that he had fathered a child so she was not shocked or surprised by my call. Sadly Joseph had died a few months before I called. I was disappointed that I had taken so long to pursue what I always felt was a missing link in my life's story. I always wondered and wanted to know who my father was; what he was like, and did I look like him? What were his interests, hobbies, did he want to know what I looked like and did he ever want to see and know me? But now I had missed the opportunity to meet him in person. I was given his medical history and information I was seeking,

16

photographs and details about his career, all the things I always desired to know and tried to figure out on my own. His wife offered to have me meet all their grown children if they were interested and willing to do so. All five of my "kid" brothers and their wives or girlfriends decided they wanted to get together and my wife Charlotte and I met them at a restaurant in Charlotte for an afternoon. I was sad that I had waited so long to act on my desire to find and to try meet my birth father in person and that I had missed talking with him by just a few months before he died. I made that important phone call that I had wanted to for years just a tad too late. I had wrestled with the decision to try to find him for years before I acted on it and now had missed the opportunity.

When Joseph learned from Emma that she was pregnant, he asked her to marry him but she declined. I always wondered why they didn't marry and the answer was easy. All I had to do was ask the source! In the 1930's and '40's and even in the '50's, having a child out of wedlock was not socially acceptable and a cause for shame for the individuals involved, the family name, the parents, and the child. Emma's decision was to leave the area and spend time with her Aunt and Uncle in Pennsylvania until the baby was born. I was born in the Williamsport, PA hospital on August 8, 1940.

A few weeks later I was taken to my new home on Emerson Street to spend my childhood years with my grandparents until we moved from there when I was 14 years old. Emma and her sister Erma left for California soon after I was born and were gone for an extended period of time. Erma eventually moved to Bellingham, WA to work at Boeing Aviation which built aircraft for the war effort. Emma worked in California at another aviation corporation during this same period of time. I did not know anything about my birth mother and her living and working in California until I was 11 years old. It was a heartbreaking time for me when I found this out as at first I felt abandoned by my mother and then angry and finally wishing that she and my birth father had married. That's the thought process of an 11-year-old.

In 6th grade I discovered who my birth mother was when my teacher, who knew the Buehler's, asked me many questions about members of the family, where they were, and what they were doing, etc.

My answers, based on my understanding of who was who in the family did not make any sense to her and she let me know I did not have my facts right. I went home that day and began asking questions based on this encounter and I learned from Gram that my family was a bit different than I thought it was up until this time in my life. Can you even imagine a teacher pursuing that line of questioning and then telling her student he doesn't have the correct information? Perhaps that is one of the myriad of reasons I pursued a career in education. Prior to this enlightenment at Elementary School #43, I was always told, understood and believed Emma (my birth mother) was my 'sister' and Paul (my mother's brother) was my 'brother' (probably because he was only 8 years older than I was). Fritz (my mother's brother) was 'Uncle Fritz' and Erma (my mother's sister) was 'Aunt Erma' and if this wasn't enough, my 'Mom and Dad' were my grandparents (they legally adopted me when I was 7 years old)! Confusing to say the least! No wonder the veteran teacher who had taught several members of the Buehler family thought I was confused. I just didn't know "the real story."

As I tried to sort all of this all out, I asked Gram why my mother and birth father didn't get married. From Gram's perspective, she told me that they were of different religious beliefs and traditions and couldn't marry out of their religious faith. When my Mom was in her 80's I shared Gram's explanation to me when I was a child about never marrying and her response was, "Nonsense, I just didn't want to marry him and I didn't want to be married." My mother was a very independent lady and I am sure did not want to be told what she could and could not do by anyone.

On June 24, 1947 an order of adoption was issued to Fred and Helen Buehler and they became, in addition to my grandparents, my parents! I was six years of age, Fred was 65 years old and Helen was 52! This was an amazing act of love, commitment, and caring! My world changed once again. My 'uncles' Paul and Fritz became my legal brothers although I did not know all of this until I was 11 years old. Also with the adoption, 'Aunt' Erma became my legal 'sister' while my 'sister' Emma became my second mother. At the age of 11, I now had two persons to call Mom and a 'brother' Paul who was now Uncle Paul. The missing uncle and other

18

'brother' Eugene was never discussed and I did not know why until 60 years later after an extended search. But I'm getting way ahead of my story...stay tuned!

We Were Just Kids

Roy Hill was a bully. I know because the only thing that I could eat for several days was soup after he punched me in the chops. Disaster struck when we were out on the playground at the furthest baseball diamond during gym class. I was 11 years old and in the sixth grade at school #43. Our gym (this was before gym magically changed somehow to PE) teacher was watching the girls play softball at the diamond closest to the school. Roy was a big kid. He was strong, tall and by far the largest student weight-wise in the school. He already had had his turn at bat and was impatient and wanted to bat again even though there were several other kids who had not had their turn. Big Roy walked up, grabbed the bat out of the boy's hands that was next in line and proceeded to order the pitcher to throw the ball to him. I walked up to Big Roy and told him that he was not being fair, that it was Billy's turn and he just had no choice other than to wait until everyone in the lineup had batted. I faintly remember him saying something to the effect, "What are you going to do about it?"

I grabbed the bat from Roy with both hands and yanked it away. I stood there in front of him and it was precisely at that moment that I tasted blood in my mouth and literally saw flashing lights and stars as blood ran down on my shirt. An important rule of nature when facing a wild beast is not to turn and run but rather to stand your ground. If perchance you run, it means you are in fear for your life and the wild beastie knows this and will chase you down and the result will not be pretty. As I glared at Roy, I started swinging the bat at him. He took off running across the field toward the teacher. Roy must have known somehow that I was not afraid to use it if I caught him. I ran as fast as

I could with one good leg and one gimpy one and the gym teacher saw us coming and started running toward the two of us. Roy survived the chase. He reached the teacher just as I was wildly swinging the bat trying to hit him on his legs as we were crossing the field. Both of us were promptly taken to the principal's office and she called my grandmother at work. When Gram arrived there was a fairly short conference between the principal and her and then I was driven home. Roy never bothered me again for the rest of the year nor did he pick on other kids when I was in the general vicinity. This incident was an important life lesson for me in many ways. I realized then, as well as now: what is right is right, what is fair is fair, and someone always has to stand up for the underdog even though it may be accompanied by a lot of pain. There was more pain to come over the years.

Early elementary school was enjoyable even though I had and still have a language processing problem as well as unique spelling abilities that are not recognized by anyone else. I was the teacher's darling pet reader in first and second grade and was called upon to read when the principal visited our class. What the teacher perhaps did not realize was that I had simply memorized Dick and Jane's Adventures by listening to her as she read each page for the class. My memory and recall has served me well over the years but unfortunately it had little effect on my spelling prowess. I took violin lessons in fifth grade and in sixth grade was in the orchestra and was even invited to play in the citywide orchestra. I really have no natural or innate musical talent. Playing the violin was purely another mechanical memory exercise as I was able to read notes and play them even though I am sure I am tone deaf.

I met with the school counselor on a few occasions, perhaps she was a school psychologist or social worker, I don't really know. I wonder if it was simply a coincidence that after these visits and friendly chats that I was asked by my classroom teacher, Miss Price, if I wanted to go into the third grade classrooms and play the violin for the students. Miss Price also gave me the opportunity to tell the class about a trip that my grandparents took me on during the previous summer. She was most patient with my nervousness and stuttering. The more enthusiastic I became telling about the experience and showing the class souvenirs that I had, the less I stuttered. Miss Price ran a tight ship and she had some rough boys to contend with, teach, and discipline. One time three of us were in the boys' bath room having a contest to see who could pee to the highest spot on the wall above the urinals when we heard a loud voice bellowing behind us, "Boys!" It was Miss Price in the boys' bathroom! We couldn't believe it! Miss Price walked into the boy's bathroom! We scrubbed and scrubbed and scrubbed the bathroom that day after school. Teachers had a way to work their magic in mysterious and sometimes wondrous ways that students remember for the rest of their lives!

City elementary schools housed students K-6 and all the high schools were organized to serve students in grades 7-12. The neighborhood high school that I was scheduled to attend was Jefferson. My grandmother, in her wisdom, went to the district's central office and somehow managed to have my high school assignment changed to John Marshall. The back story here is that all of her children, which included my mother, her brothers Eugene, Fritz, Paul and her sister Erma, had attended Jefferson. I am sure the name Eugene Buehler would have been readily recognized by the staff and faculty and it would not have been in my best interest to attend Jefferson. What a turn of events the future held for me…the first teaching assignment of my career was at that very school!

In seventh grade at Marshall, I worked very hard at becoming a serious academic student. I carried a briefcase, always polished my shoes, and wore dress pants and shirt…never dungarees. I had average grades in junior high but beginning in ninth grade my reading and language processing problem was something that I simply could not overcome. Actually I felt like a dumb kid academically when I received my report cards but I knew I was smart. I managed to graduate with a Regents diploma and achieved it by attending summer school. I am sure my graduation was based as much on my personality than my grade point average. I found my old year book and under my name it read: Stamp Club 3; FTA 3,4; Audio Visual 1,2,3,4; Service Corps 3,4; Marshal Day 3; Memorial Scholarship Drive 3,4; Memorial Day Parade 2; Treasurer of the FTA 4, Dance Committee 2,3; Summer School Office Help 2; Wrestling 1; and under my senior picture it read, "It was Greek to me."

I was a friend to all and was able to move effortlessly between the various cliques in the school. Mr. Vetter was my social studies teacher and I really enjoyed him, his teaching style, and humor and was able to sign up for his classes every year from my freshman to senior year. I had an inkling that perhaps I would like someday to teach and many of the girls that I was friendly with were involved in the Future Teachers of America (FTA) Club and invited me to attend a meeting. Since I was the only male in the Club I enjoyed the gatherings and all the related activities. During your senior year, if you were an FTA member, you could actually be a student teacher if a faculty member wished to sponsor you. I served as a student teacher in Mrs. Havill's science class during the whole of my senior year. It is strange how things work out and what fate awaits us... Twelve years later I was the Director of Science for all the K-12 schools in the City of Rochester, and Mrs. Havill was at that time, the Science Department Head at Marshall, and I was her supervisor. In my first meeting with all the Department Heads in the District I answered a question she asked and I responded, "Yes, Mrs. Havill, I..." She stopped me mid-sentence and said, "My first name is Jean, please call me by that name." And I replied, "Thank you Mrs. Havill, I will." I was a bit embarrassed but somehow my brain just couldn't get the right words to come out. I guess I provided a bit of entertainment for the meeting that day.

My grandmother always insisted that I attend church which, as a 14-year-old, was the last thing that I really wanted to do until one Sunday I noticed a new girl in a pew with her Mom that I hadn't seen before. She was very pretty with long black hair, a wonderful personality, and she had a beautiful smile. She was darn cute with a figure to match and I was enchanted. After this chance meeting, Grandma had no problem encouraging me to attend church. I learned that her name was Kay and where she lived. It was a small congregation with an active young people's group and so from time to time we saw each other at various church functions. She was a beauty and little did I know then that she was to become an important part of my life.

While in high school one of my best friends was George Horeth, a refugee from Germany, whose family suffered through World War II. They immigrated first to Canada and then to the US and Rochester in 1948. George and I became fast friends and in our senior year we vowed to travel the country together and go to California after graduation. Since I was involved in the FTA, my guidance counselor suggested that I might be interested in the 3-1-1-1 program at the State University of New York at Brockport. It was an accelerated program designed to prepare teachers to enter the profession. With a full schedule of classes each semester and attending three summer sessions, one could graduate in three years and be fully certified to teach. I applied for the program and was accepted. I was 17 years old when I graduated from high school and started college.

Attending the first summer session I lived in a fraternity house with 24 other guys. I wasn't ready for the freedom I had or being on my own but somehow I made it through the summer and during the fall semester I majored in card playing at the frat house and financed my weekend fun with money I had won playing poker. Just before the Christmas break of the fall semester, the Dean called me into his office to inform me that I would not be invited back for the spring semester. While I was at SUNY, George and I stayed in touch and he would drive out to the college on weekends for a little hell rising. We agreed that our initial plan of taking off for California after high school seemed like an even better plan now that I would not be going back to college in January. We decided to save our money and I secured a job at Ridge Lumber Company driving a truck and delivering loads of lumber. An opportunity to make more money presented itself with a job offer at DynaColor Corporation, working in a low light environment with a team operating large machinery coating photographic paper. George and I planned that in February we would both quit our jobs and leave for California. During the time I was working, Kay was attending a private high school in Houghton, NY. Since I was working, I had my own car and would drive down to Houghton every weekend to see her. It was her senior year and I told her that I was going to California for awhile with George while she finished out her senior year.

Before Christmas arrived George had received his third speeding ticket and lost his driver's license. To his way of thinking he felt that without his license he had lost all of his freedom and, in addition, he wasn't comfortable with me being the only one able to drive on our trip. This prompted him to visit an Army recruiting office and he signed up right on the spot on his first visit and called me that evening. He told me about his court appearance the evening before in which he had his license taken away and he was not going to California but instead he had joined the Army. I was stunned. He tried to talk me into going into the Army with him but it didn't seem like a good idea for me. Ironically George spent his time in the Army stationed in Germany and he spoke the language!

I had already given notice and quit my job so I packed up and headed across the country, first to the state of Washington to spend some time on Orcus Island in Puget Sound, and then down the coast to Southern California staying a few weeks in Carlsbad. After that I traveled into Mexico, then back across the southern part of the country to Florida where I spent a few weeks in St. Petersburg, and finally returning to New York State before my money ran out. My travels covered a period of months. During the time I was away I was sending postcards to Kay all along the way and she had a map of the United States on the wall of her dorm room and was tracking my postcards and the routes I was traveling with stick pins on the map.

Of the many experiences and adventures I had on the cross-country road trip two of them stand out in my mind. One was spending an overnight in jail in Midland, Texas. I was driving over the speed limit on a new section of a four lane highway late at night when the 60mph speed limit changed to 40mph and I didn't notice. When I was stopped, with New Mexico plates on the car and asked where I lived, where I was coming from, where I was going, none of my answers made any sense to the officer. Right then and there I was presented with the back seat of the police car. My car was towed. While in the interrogation room, officers were going through my car and noticed the mandatory Mexico entry inspection sticker on the windshield. This may have caused them to come up with creative bad thoughts or ideas about why I had gone to

Mexico. To add to all the suspicions the police had the fact that I had New Mexico license plates on the car didn't help a bit. My New York plates had expired on January 30th and I wanted to have the car legally registered which I took care of when I was in Santa Fe. When I was in California I painted the car blue with red and yellow flames on the front fenders. The problem with this was that the registration listed the color of the car as red which it was before I painted it. Nothing added up to make sense for the police. I was allowed one phone call but the officer did not give me the phone, instead he asked for the number and then dialed it. When he asked for the number, I gave him my grandmother's home number and when he called he was told by the operator that it was no longer a working number. I was at a loss for words or an explanation. He tried a second time. Same result.

Unknown to me while I was on the road, Gram's old phone number, Greenwood 8-488 (GR8-488) had been changed by the phone company because they switched from operator switchboards to automatic dialing with new phone numbers assigned to each customer. Nothing added up for the police or made sense to them especially the non-working phone number. The officers took my finger prints, then my belt, shoe laces, everything in my pockets and walked me to a cell and slammed the door. The next morning they received confirmation from the Greece Police that indeed I did live at 55 Laura Drive with my Grandmother and they released me. I went to my car in the parking lot where I found everything in the suitcase had been dumped in the trunk, the spare tire dismounted, the air cleaner from the engine also in the trunk, and the front seat removed from the car. I guess they were searching for drugs? I went back into the building a bit hot under the collar to object to what they had done to my car and the Sergeant told me the best advice he could give me was to get in the car right now, get out of town, and never come back to Midland, Texas or even look back in the rear view mirror. That scared the 'begesus' out of me and I was quickly on my way and driving 40 miles per hour. I've driven through Midland twice over the years since then and I carefully observed the speed limit each time!

The more significant experience on that road trip was sitting on the rim of the Grand Canyon before sunrise and watching the sunlight slowly highlighting the layers of red rocks of the canyon walls. It was almost a spiritual experience for me and I felt very small as well as lonely. I thought…all this beauty…and I'm here alone. I want to share this experience with someone. I knew sharing it would make it so much more meaningful. I sat there a long time until the canyon was in full color. I now have a wonderful travel partner and have had the same friend for 55 years and counting and it only gets better with each trip, each sunrise, and each sunset. I am blessed.

When I returned home in April/May it was close to Kay's graduation and we began seeing much more of each other. I started working in the drafting department at Pfaulder Company. Kay was 17 years old when she graduated in June and we planned that as soon as she turned 18, which would have been on the 25th of July, we would elope and get married in a state that did not require parent permission and signature. I told my Grandmother about my plans so she would not worry that I had taken off again and she made it clear that planning to elope was not the right thing to do nor was it considerate of the families and of others. In a very short period of time Kay's mother was informed about our plans to elope. Both our families planned a church wedding for us. On July 30, 1960, five days after Kay s birthday we were married. We were just two kids, 18 and 20, young, naive and ready to take on the world.

Postscript: Our first daughter Tonja was born on June 5, 1961, 11 months later which ended all the conjecture floating around the biosphere about our quickly planned and executed marriage.

Post-Postscript: The reader may notice a name change in the following stories. Kay and Charlotte are one in the same person. Charlotte's birth certificate reads, Charlotte Kathryn Morris and as a child and young adult everyone called her Kay. In 1980 she received her Master's degree from Alfred University and when asked what name she wished to have printed on her diploma, she indicated Charlotte K. Buehler. From that time on, everyone, including me, called her Charlotte with just a few exceptions; her Mom, brother, sister and a few old friends who only knew her as Kay. It was Kay from 1942-1980 and professionally it has always been Charlotte.

Finding Our Way

"Either you can pull the 'rip cord' and I'll start it or you can start it and I'll pull the 'rip cord'." This was pretty much our first conversation as newlyweds in the parking lot of the church at the conclusion of our wedding and following the reception. Our second conversation as we drove out off was, "Were you able to fix the windshield wipers this morning and get them to work?" "You know it's going to rain?" Our honey moon and married life started out in a hot rod 1950 Ford with a big Oldsmobile engine that I put in it for power and racing and it was our only means of transportation. It took two people to start the engine. There was no room for the solenoid to fit on the starter motor with the converted engine and I had run a wire cable from the starter motor lever up to and attach it behind the front bumper of the car. With one person kneeling down to reach and then pull the cable which engaged the starter and with the other person in the front seat, s/he would be able to push the starter button on the dash and the engine would roar to life. An excellent starting alternative to this procedure was to park the Ford on a steep incline or hill and let it roll down and when sufficient speed was attained, let the clutch out while the car was in gear and it would usually start. Well most of the time it would start except on very cold mornings, when it was raining, or when the incline wasn't steep or long enough.

I pulled the 'rip cord' and Charlotte hit the starter button and we were off on our honeymoon. We traveled to a tiny and almost unfurnished cottage nestled among dozens of others at Delta Lake Camp in the foothills of the mountains. After an overnight and a day or two, we drove further up into the Adirondacks stopping for another night or two at old and inexpensive 1930's and '40's styled motels found along those mountain routes. I managed to get a speeding ticket on the way home which took all the remaining money we had left that we had received as gifts at our reception. We were dead broke but not in the exact same way Hillary stated it when she quipped, "We were dead broke when we left the White House." There is broke and then there is really broke! We were the latter.

Returning to our apartment in Charlotte near the Lake, we settled into married life and began adjusting to our independent ways. I think I have finally gotten over not having the top put back on the tube of tooth paste. I am positive Charlotte's adjustments have been colossal and surely are not quite finished yet! Our love nest was the upper floor of a house and the family below that owned it was Italian. The husband never spoke English while, at the same time, his wife was pleased to have us as newlyweds and took us both under her wing. She offered us tomatoes from their garden and garlic which hung drying in their garage and taught us how to make sauce from scratch. The smell of her cooking permeated our apartment day after day when she was preparing meals and we were instantly ravenous when arriving home after work. In the fall, the smell of new wine fermenting filled the apartment. One evening Charlotte cut her hand badly while washing a glass coffee pot which had broken in the dish pan. I panicked as is my usual practice when there is a lot of blood and we wrapped her hand in a towel and ran downstairs for help. Our landlords took wonderful care of us, first cleaning the wound and then bandaging it, followed by a full water glass tumbler of new wine from the oak barrel in the cellar. The pain of the deep cut quickly dissipated and the challenge to climb the stairs home became the remaining focus for that evening.

It was at that apartment I began to learn what not to say. I'm still learning by the way. Charlotte baked my absolute favorite cake for my birthday. "So what do you think about the pineapple upside down cake I made?" "It is good, very good, but doesn't taste quite like my grandmother's." I think twenty-five years passed slowly before I ever had another pineapple upside down cake for my birthday! And if you can believe it, I've said even dumber things over the more than five decades of living with my best friend and soul mate. She is loving and patient, kind and understanding, and bakes heavenly pineapple upside down cakes, but hasn't forgotten my commentary. I haven't either!

Our apartment was located at the end of the street and close to the top of a small hill. Each morning I would let the Ford roll down the street and bring the engine to life by letting the clutch out when sufficient speed was attained and then I was off to work at the Pfaulder Company. Leaving the parking lot at the end of the day was always an interesting challenge as I had to find someone to volunteer to push the starter button while I did my one knee prayer position rip cord act by the front bumper. This always led to questions and conversations in the cafeteria the following day especially when there was a downpour the previous day.

My work assignment at Pfaulder was to make photostatic copies of blueprints for the engineering department, pull them from files and then re-file them. I was very good at this as I quickly memorized the seven digit system and codes. Upon completion of the printed photostatic copies and blueprints, I delivered them throughout the plant to the various departments and foremen. I was intrigued with the design and engineering work completed by engineers and I had a little knowledge of what they were doing from drafting classes that I took while in high school. I also had a friend, Larry, who was my age and he worked as a draftsman in the engineering department and I decided that was what I wanted to do for a career. I spoke with a senior engineer whom I respected and he encouraged me to pursue my dream but told me I needed to go to school and get an education and a degree. I made an appointment with the person who had hired me in the Personnel Department and asked him if I could have an opportunity to move into the drafting department. It was made clear to me that was not going to happen and if I wanted to pursue that path the only way for that to happen was to get a degree first, and then he would consider a possible reassignment. I contemplated my options and I thought the quickest way to achieve my goal was to attend school on a full-time basis rather than drag it out over several years in order to get a college degree which would allow me to move into the drafting department. I've always been a very impatient person.

We had been married just a year when these thoughts were fermenting in my brain and we had baby girl Tonja plus a brand new VW to pay for and I was not making very much money. Charlotte was so supportive of this crazy idea I had that she said she would find a job so I would be able go to college. It was August and every university I called told me registration for full-time students for the fall semester had closed and that I could apply for the next year to see if I would be accepted. Wait a whole year? Bold and not knowing any better, I made a personal appointment to meet with the President of Roberts Wesleyan College (RWC).I had never been to the campus and I certainly did not know the President but I had a goal and wanted an opportunity to try college again. I must have convinced him somehow since he told me that with classes starting in two weeks he was going to take a chance on me and I was, at the conclusion of the appointment with him, a full-fledged member of the freshman class. He called the Dean and told him I was coming right over to his office to meet with him and to register! This even after I told him I had flunked out of SUNY Brockport! It was a miracle! President Voller remembered me and our meeting and conversation when he shook my hand and handed me my diploma five years later.

I gave my two week notice at Pfaulder but we needed to find a place to live on campus as a full-time student. A friend of the family had a small sixteen foot camping trailer he towed behind his car on vacations and offered to let us use it from September until May. At that time the RWC campus had a mobile home park for married couples so we were able to rent a space and set the trailer up on campus. Charlotte found a position at Busch and Lomb and, later that year in the spring, we moved to an apartment in Rochester. We had a baby sitter for Tonja and one evening after work when we arrived home she called her sitter Mommy Dorothy and that was too much for both of us to take. We realized this was not a good situation and we wanted something better for all of us, so we decided Charlotte would quit her job and I would find work so she could be a stay-at-home mother. I applied at General Motors, Rochester

Products Division (RPD) and was immediately hired as an hourly employee for more money than I had ever made in my life. The high hourly rate of pay was because RPD was an AFL-CIO United Auto Workers (UAW) union manufacturing plant. My membership in the UAW was not to last very long but I did not know this when I started working in the plant.

My work schedule was six days a week with overtime on the 3:30-midnight shift and I scheduled my classes starting at 8:00am finishing at 2:00pm. My first week at work I was assigned to a metal degreasing machine to operate and there was a lot of down time. It was boring waiting for the machine to go through its cleaning cycle so I operated three machines at once on different schedules to keep busy and make the time go by quickly. At the end of the second day my co-workers and the union rep met with me and told me to slow down and that I was making everyone else look bad. Silly me, I didn't heed the warning and on Friday my foreman told me that I had to stop operating three machines as I had created a safety concern for the department. Monday when I showed up for work and went to punch in at the time clock, my foreman was waiting for me and he walked me through the plant to the front office complex and left me there to speak to the Director of the Personnel Department. After a long discussion about my plans for the future he offered me a salary position in Production Control, assigned an electric scooter for my use, and told me that I needed to wear a white shirt and tie to work and I would also receive an increase in pay if I was interested in the position. Are you kidding me? My planning, ordering and work area was an enclosed glass office complete with air conditioning that sat in the middle of the unbearably hot factory and I enjoyed that position assignment until I graduated. One side of the office windows looked out over the department where I had been working just the week before. The excellent salary allowed us to pay my tuition, move to an apartment complex in Rochester, and have enough money to buy three new vehicles during my college years, enjoy my racing and car hobby, enjoy vacations, and have everything our growing family needed and desired.

In the last semester of my senior year I needed to take an advanced math course to complete my major, comprehensive sciences, meaning attaining minors in all the science offerings as well as in mathematics. The one course I needed was only taught in the evening and did not fit with my work hours at GM. Crazy as it seems…remember my appointment with President Volley?…I set up an appointment with the math professor and explained my dilemma and asked if my spouse Charlotte attended every class in my place and took notes and if I did all the class assignments and exams, would he allow me to enroll in his course? Amazingly he agreed with the stipulation that I had to take the mid-term and final exams in his classroom with all the other students. I agreed. Charlotte thankfully agreed also and attended every class, took copious notes which were excellent and which I studied along with the text book, and I completed all assignments and then Charlotte delivered them each class meeting to Professor Rose. Charlotte was amazing! Her notes were wonderful and only with her attendance, insights, and notes, was I able to ace the course as well as the mid-term and final. Now if that isn't love and dedication, I don't know what is! Years have gone by and I haven't thanked her recently…Honey, Thank YOU and I think you should have gotten college credit also for the course!

When I graduated I decided I wanted to teach in an inner-city school rather than stay with GM. By the time I graduated our second daughter, Tammy had joined the Buehler family. As I walked across the stage to receive my diploma I heard loud and clear, Tammy's small voice in the audience crying out, "That's my Daddy!"

It wasn't a difficult decision to decide what career I now wanted; it was just a bit complicated. My time at GM was rewarding in terms of salary but that's all. I looked around at what my future might be if I stayed; no money problems but on call and owned by the company, or a move to Detroit to another GM factory—and all my supervisors and positions that I might move into those folks either had a problem with alcohol, health issues, or family/marriage due to job demands and pressures. When I indicated to my boss that I would be leaving at the end of the year upon graduation, I received a raise. I turned in my notice in writing a few months later, another raise. I thought I better check with Kodak and Xerox just to be sure I was making the right decision. Kodak offered the same salary as GM for a sales position in the mid-west which required being on the road. Xerox offered more money for a second shift foreman's position in manufacturing. I had a choice of several teaching positions and accepted the one in the Rochester City School District at Jefferson High School for $5,480 year, one third of the salary I was earning at GM. We never looked back and as it turns out, it was an excellent decision for us but unrealized for some time and not fully appreciated until later in life.

I often think now how different our life's story might have been if we had not followed our hearts and not chosen the education career path. Who knows? I was fortunate to have choices as well as many helping hands, friends, mentors, and opportunities on our journey; the most important of all was Charlotte!

The Way Forward

After the school had been evacuated, the students were sent home and not allowed to reenter the building. The fire trucks were still in the street and firemen were swarming throughout the upper floors of the building. I was sitting alone in the faculty room at Jefferson High School contemplating the day's events and trying to figure out how I was going to explain what had happened and more importantly, the "why" of it all. Suddenly the Principal, followed closely behind by the Vice Principal, burst into the faculty room and confronted me with, "What's this I hear about tear gas?" I looked up and saw tears flowing down the cheeks of both Mr. Morreale and Mr. Van Delinder and I could feel an uncontrollable smile beginning to form uncontrollably on my face. This was not the best thing to be occurring at this serious moment but I could barely contain myself. Yes, bromoacetone (common name, tear gas) does make one's eyes flow tears uncontrollably and they stood over me with tears running down their faces.

This episode occurred in June but the seeds for the incident had been planted the previous September. I was a new science teacher and as an ancient administrative practice usually dictates, the most challenging students are assigned to the newest teachers in the school perhaps as a test to see if they can make it through their first few probationary years. There was a group of seniors that needed one credit in a science course in order to graduate. Each senior had taken and failed the required 9th grade general science course. Many of them had taken it again when they were in 10th grade and failed it once again. Several members of the Jefferson HS football team were included in the group of seniors needing a credit in science in order to graduate. I was politely "asked" or, I should

35

say, assigned to teach these students the 9th grade general science course once again in their senior year. In discussions with my department head I was able to convince them to allow me to change the curriculum to be taught from general science to a course in chemistry. This was only approved on the condition that all the students would take the City-wide final exam in June. This exam was one developed and written by representatives of all the chemistry teachers from each one of the District's high schools. This year-end exam would then be considered a standardized measure of achievement of scholarship for all students enrolled in the course in all city high schools and in the course I would teach. This course of study was referred to as Chemistry (Chem.) 11 by both the City School District and the State.

All the enrolled students including the football players needing the one science credit showed up for class the first day of school. I told them if they worked with me and did what I asked them to do, that they would all pass chemistry, be eligible to graduate, and in the process we would have some fun along the way. They responded by telling me that they had heard from other students who had already taken the class, that Chem. 11 was a tough course and they would not be able to pass it. I assured them that they all would do all right and graduate BUT they had to do everything in class that I asked them to do. As an aside comment I jokingly said, "…and if you don't do what I ask you to do, I'll have you down on your hands and knees begging for mercy." There was a lot of hooting, hollering, and laughter from the championship team members about my braggadocio commentary and challenge. "We're tough; we'll never beg, never have and never will! We're Jefferson football players and we are tough!" "There is nothing you can do to make us get down on our hands and knees." I left it at that as it was just a figure of speech and my way of having a little fun with them.

It turned out to be a great year! They loved the "hands-on" labs and begged me to schedule more for them which I did. Class attendance, homework assignments, good class behavior, attending class on time seemed to be an issue with this group with their other subject area teachers. This was not a problem with me in the Chem. 11 class as I had developed a "currency system" of rewards and "payday" was scheduled every Friday. I had the shop class print all the denominations of paper currency with my picture on each one of the bills. They quickly became known as "Buehler Bucks." Instead of posting grades in the record book on Fridays, they received their "pay checks" in sealed envelopes in the amount they had earned that week from quizzes, class attendance/behavior, homework, and lab work, etc. and this "dollar" amount was recorded in lieu of a letter or numerical grade based on the posted conversion chart on the bulletin board. Of course a team is a team and I know that a few dollars from various paychecks may have been shared, bartered or borrowed from fellow class members for totals to be turned in for each marking period report cards. For the marking period, I posted the amount of money required that had to be turned in to me for an A, B, C, or D letter grade for their report cards as per Jefferson's grading policy. I had them keep their money, to be turned in as a way of creating increased interest and responsibility for their work and effort.

Following the first marking period the principal and department head requested that I meet with them to explain why there were so many A's and B's on the students' report cards and no failing grades at all. My explanation and rationalization for the paper currency grading system, pay checks, and pay days caused their eyes to glaze over and I was turned loose once again with a verbal notice that the final City-wide exam results and final grades for the year for the class would be carefully monitored and reviewed by them.

The school year flew by and before I knew it June had arrived. I assured my students that they were ready for the big final City exam. As a class, we had been practicing taking old exams from the previous years in class and I told them they were well prepared for any question that they would be asked. I pleaded with them to just think, take their time and remember their labs, formulas, and explanations they had written in their lab books for each experiment and chemical reaction. I then wished them all good luck that now it was exam time and the year has ended and this was the last time I'd see them until graduation in two weeks. As soon as the words left my mouth, I heard from the back of the room from the student I'd given the nick-name Big Mike. "Hey Mr. B, remember the first day of class when you told us you'd have us down on our hands and knees begging for mercy?" "Well, we never begged you for anything and the year is over and you can't make us beg you for anything anymore because today is the last day of class for the year!"

"Well I do have one last lab prepared for you but it will be a demonstration lab that I will perform for all of you." I held my breath as I poured a small quantity of acetone into the test tube which contained a small quantity of bromine, held it for a moment over the Bunsen burner, saw it change from a deep red colored liquid to clear and then poured the colorless liquid onto some paper towels on the demo lab table in the front of the classroom to allow it to evaporate. Then quickly I walked out into the hall and closed the door. Standing outside I could hear what was going on in the room. "What was that for?" "Did you see THAT?" "He changed that from a red solid to clear water and poured it on the paper towels." "Can you smell that?" "I don't smell anything." "Here, smell these paper towels." "Open the windows!" "Open all the windows, tops and bottoms!" "My eyes are watering!" "Open all the windows!" "Get rid of those paper towels!"

I just assumed that the students had thrown the paper towels out the window and right after school I planned that I would go out and pick them up. Wrong! I opened the classroom door, I took my last deep breath of fresh air, held it and walked in and closed the door behind me. I didn't see the paper towels in the wastepaper basket, on the lab table under the venting hood, or on the floor so I thought I was right in guessing they went out the window. "Hey Mr. B, we are begging you for mercy...let us out of here even though the bell hasn't rung!" I responded, "Are you down on your hands and knees?" All together, in loud voices I heard, "No." I responded sarcastically, "Well?" At which point I heard, "OK, Mr. B, we are all down on our knees!"

Since this was the last period of the day and I thought I had planned this perfectly, I opened the door just few minutes before the end of class bell rang and told them to go very quietly to their lockers and I'd see them in the gym for final exams next week. It seemed to be a perfectly executed "got you". It would be our little secret class joke ending our great year together and would be something for them to remember from their senior year and Chem. 11!

It was not to be a well kept class secret for very long. What I did not realize when I was out in the hall was that the students disposed of the paper towels by tossing them into the opening of the large re-circulation fresh air return in the room which immediately distributed bromoacetone fumes throughout the entire school through the ventilation system of ducts to all the classrooms in the entire school. Someone on the first floor near the office pulled the fire alarm and the school was immediately evacuated and the City Fire Department automatically called and they responded post haste. Sadly that was the ending of my little class "got-you."

Post script: All members of the class graduated that year. The lowest score for all members of this Chem. 11 class on the City-wide exam was an 83! I think their success was the only thing that kept me from being terminated at the end of that school year. I was hoping that this event would soon be forgotten but not to be. Mr. Morrale with his sense of humor made it a point in his comments to the graduating class in his speech to say, "…and Mr. B has promised not to do any more tear gas experiments next year." I taught at Jefferson HS for 5 years while sponsoring the senior class through their HS years beginning when they were freshman. I was honored to have the senior class dedicate their yearbook to me.

In 1970 a group of parents were interested in starting an alternative school for their children so I was one of the first to volunteer to join this "experiment" and adventure. I had an "interview" with Dr. David Youst sitting in the front seat of his white Chevy convertible with the top down in front of Jefferson HS in June. David had been employed by Eastman Kodak and was hired by the District to design, staff, and open a new and unique "learner-centered" Junior High School in Rochester. The school was under the auspices of the City School District and the Board of Education but the oversight, curriculum and operational regulations of the school was designed to operate under the direct control of a group of parents, the Board of Directors, and the Program Director, Dr. David Youst.

I remember my interview with David Youst in front of Jefferson High School. Beyond the standard expected questions about training, experiences, thoughts about schools, and teaching, which I answered, I also shared the story about Buehler Bucks. David was very interested and asked me to tell him more. I shared the making of an actual erosion stream table with students, model glaciers with real ice, rocks, and dirt, independent senior science projects, which included building a working Van de Graff generator to make ozone, raising lab mice, and taking students on field trips on weekends to various geologic sites in the State.

I told him about a student I had named Mike who built the Van de Graff generator. Mike started out with me by signing up for an independent study class I was offering for all students who had successfully completed all the science courses the school offered. Mike had completed his Regents Physics class and wanted to do more work in that area of interest. I suggested several projects and he became fascinated with the possibility of building a Van de Graff generator. In the old monster or Frankenstein movies, the tower of high voltage consisting of two steel rods with lighting-like electricity moving up the wires, that is created by a Van de Graff generator. To build the one Mike created, he had to learn how to run a lathe in the shop class to spin the coil of wire which consisted of hundreds of wrappings, build a power source which consisted of finding an old neon sign and dismantling it to use the transformer, and a dozen other new skills needed. After he built a working generator, he demonstrated it to students in my science classes. It was a very impressive demonstration! He would hold a florescent light tube in his hands and it would flicker on as he stood ten feet away from the machine. He also would demonstrate the power of static electricity by having the blue streak of electricity jump from the generator to his hand and back as his hair stood on end as he was charged. The students were more than impressed!

Demonstrations can only last so long and the school year was far from over when Mike completed building the Van de Graff. One of the by-products of operating the generator is Ozone. Ozone is the fresh smell you sense in the air after a severe thunder storm in the summer. The high charge of static electricity allows oxygen with two molecules to pick up third molecule thereby changing oxygen into ozone. Ozone has various effects on living things and not all are positive. As Mike's research and reading continued on, he wanted to conduct some experiments using ozone. I suggested he might want to use lab mice in his experiments as it can have a few negative effects on humans. Mike built a Plexiglas box to collect ozone while running the generator while mice were in the box breathing the ozone. I taught Mike about experimental and control groups, observations, hypothesis and null-hypothesis, record keeping and various scientific method procedures. Shortly thereafter Mike had two groups of white lab mice in cages in the science store room which was attached to my classroom. The hypothesis that we developed was that mice exposed to ozone would lose their appetite and therefore lose weight. This met careful record keeping, weighing, accurate food amounts, careful timing of exposures to ozone and a host of other variables. The end result of a school year of experimentation resulted in Mike finding out that mice exposed to ozone for 15 minutes a day not only results in increased appetites, food consumption, and weight gain, but also in breeding. Meaning more litters, more babies, more often. We were being overrun with white mice! Mike also had to come into school on weekends and all school vacations to care for his mice.

With the school year ending and Mike planning on attending the university in August, he wanted to know what to do with his lab mice which he had grown close to and cared so much about. He told me his mother would not allow him to bring them home. I suggested he might wish to call several places that might use lab mice including the Seneca Park Zoo and also offer them to students. The students, hospitals and local colleges all turned him down so he was delighted and excited to learn that the zoo was interested and would take all his mice. He wanted to know if I could drive him and his cages of mice to the zoo. Mike was creative, a deep thinker, and a wonderful student but that did not prepare him for our trip. It never occurred to me that I needed to discuss with him his gift he was making to the zoo. Little did I realize the significance and the impact of the delivery. Mike made the appointment and we delivered the cages to one of the zoo keepers where he had made arrangements. Mike wanted to see where the cages we going to be kept

41

and the employee said he didn't need the cages, the zoo had their own cages. We transferred the mice to the zoo's cages and loaded the empty cages back into the trunk of my car. Mike then asked where they would be putting his mice in the zoo for display. He was told that a few would be put a few in the snake cages on a scheduled basis. It was a long silent ride back to Jefferson that June day. Mike stopped to see me at school the following fall when he was home from Alfred and was delighted to tell me that he sold his Van de Graff generator to the Physics Department for $250.

It was getting uncomfortable sitting in the convertible in the late afternoon sun when David asked me the final question, "If I gave you a piece of string and an empty spook of thread, could you teach a science lesson?" I answered, "Yes!" To which he replied, go ahead and tell be what the lesson would be." I told him how I would teach, by way of demonstration, using that piece of string and the spool to demonstrate; centripetal and centrifugal force, speed of orbit dependant on radius and diameter of orbit, rotating mass, and gravitational 'pull'. He offered me a teaching position as we sat in the front seat and told me he better go in and speak with the principal to let him know I would not be returning in September.

The school was to open in September and at the time of my chat with David, I don't think too many other faculty or staff had been hired. It was a thrilling experience to be a part of designing and planning what was to be a new and different approach to education for students in the Rochester City School District (RCSD). The newly created school was to become known as Interim Jr. High. The name in and of itself indicates a bit of the philosophy and struggle in defining itself. The school was planned to be housed in two separate buildings on Prince Street which were the former women's dormitories of the University. It was a school without a name. The Rochester Telephone Company needed to know what the formal name of the school so they could list it in the City phone book alphabetically with all the other 45 schools in the District. A 'name your school' contest for students took place without definitive results determined before the Phone Company's deadline for submitting the book to the printers. For the interim time period and until the following year when the new phone book was to be printed, the school was simply listed as Interim JH. The contest ended and the students and faculty were determined to leave it as it had been listed the past year in the phone book and the name lasted for its entire duration of existence, even when the school was moved to another building location.

During the time I was teaching at Jefferson and Interim, we were able to purchase our first new home on Cross Gates Road where we welcomed Todd into the Buehler family. I was able to pursue my Master's degree and was awarded a National Science Foundation grant to study geology at the University of Texas in El Paso. I received a Master's in Educational Administration and a Certificate of Advance Study in Educational Administration through SUNY Brockport. While at Jefferson HS, I also taught evening adult education courses in mathematics and courses in the GED program for the District. I worked during the summers and my first job was at Turner Construction as an assistant diesel mechanic. I then did estimates and sold contracts for installing black top driveways. Following this experience, the next summer, working with a fellow faculty member and friend, we filed as a small company under the NYS Doing Business as (DBA) statute. Our enterprise was the Buehler and Pedzich (B&P) Painting and Construction Co. During the spring in the evenings I would do estimates and obtain painting and roofing contracts for the following summer for the company to complete. It seemed a bit like fun and games but almost sliding off a roof and just stopping at the edge helped us to focus on the business at hand. We had signed contracts for painting big and tall houses that I'm sure other companies would think twice about undertaking. It is much easier to pluck "the low bearing fruit" for signing contracts to paint ranch houses in the 'burbs than the ones we contracted to paint. We were hungry for summer work and we amassed enough stories about painting, roofing, and home additions to fill another book. Let's leave it at that. Well, maybe hiring your own daughter could be mentioned just in passing. We needed to paint wooden and wrought iron fences around back yards and swimming pools and Tammy still, to this day, doesn't think she got paid enough for her work.

During my early years of teaching we also were fortunate to be able to purchase some acreage in the southern tier in NYS near Cameron and we designed and built our own year-around cabin and what, we thought at the time, would be our retirement home. Our children and their friends fondly remember the outhouse during the construction phase, Tonja falling through the second floor while moving plywood to install the flooring, as well as special New Year's Eve's and vacations at the cabin with family and friends. All these wonderful memories also included tractor and wagon rides, ice skating on the pond in the winter, cutting trees, building the road, digging out the natural spring for the gravity feed water supply, the tree house, warm wood fires in the stove in middle of the winter, and toasting marshmallows outside in the summer. Then there were all the wonderful "firsts". The first meal cooked in the new kitchen, the first hot shower in the new bathroom, and the first night in the upstairs finished bedrooms, and the first fire in the wood stove that dad built and the first time we had our own electricity. So many wonderful memories!

While the building project was ongoing, back home our three children were attending the Spencerport CSD and a group of neighborhood parents had some concerns with the District's schools. In response, Charlotte and I hosted an open forum at our home designed to meet with the President of the Board of Education (BOE), the Superintendent of Schools, and the President of the Teacher's Union. This forum resulted in a discussion of issues relating to the lack of a contract between the BOE and the Teacher's Union. As a result of this gathering and discussion, a few days later I was asked by our neighbors to consider campaigning for a seat on the BOE to represent our neighborhood, families, and children. With the vision and hard work of our friends and the neighborhood parents, I was elected. It was for a 3 year term. I was also elected to serve two additional three year terms. It was a steep learning curve and I was honored to serve during my second term as the Board's Vice President and during my third term as President. While on the Board, I was still teaching in the City and the Spencerport CSD experienced a difficult, damaging, and long lasting teachers' strike during my tenure. In the early 1970's it was extremely

44

rare to have a teacher as a member of the Board but it did not seem to hamper me in any way and I was opinionated regarding child-centered education policies and curriculums. Looking back, I fondly remember a Board meeting when Joe Clement, the Superintendent, addressing me out of frustration no doubt, said, "Buehler, if you know so damn much, why aren't you a Superintendent?" Well, Joe had a very good point I hadn't considered before that moment in time.

Post Script: When I was Superintendent of the Oswego City School District, I called my good friend Joe Clement who was at the time, retired and living in Florida, and told him I needed some help and asked him to consider coming out of retirement to serve as the Assistant Superintendent of Business. Joe spent 6 months with me that year. It was delightful working together professionally and most successful for both of us. Together with the Board, we developed a challenging budget which garnered community support and approval and reduced the District's overall spending.

While still with the Rochester City School District (RCSD), I volunteered to join the Science Department at Edison Tech even though this older school was going to close in a couple of years. A new and modern Edison Tech was on the drawing boards waiting to be built. The year the new Edison opened I was there and taught part time while managing a grant at Central Office as the Project Director responsible with a team of teachers developing a new Unified Science curriculum and program. The program was field tested, copyrighted and then sold to other districts for implementation. The following year I was appointed to a full time position in Central Office to serve as Director of Science K-12 for the District. In quick succession I served as Director of the Federal Elementary and Secondary Education Act (ESEA) K-12 and then as Director of Magnet School Curriculum and Development.

My teaching career began the Rochester City School District (RCSD) at Jefferson High School in 1966. I taught at Jefferson until 1971 and from 1968-74, I taught evening Adult Education and GED at East High School. I then moved to Interim Junior High School from 1971-75. I was at Edison Technical High School (both the old school and the newly built one) 1975-77. During this same period of time, I served as Project

45

Director for the Unified Science Program grades 9-12 at Central Office. In 1977 I moved to Central Office on a full-time basis as Director of Elementary and Secondary Education Act K-12 and in 1978 was named as Director of Science K-12 for all schools in the City. Then in 1979 I was named as the Director of Magnet School Curriculum and Development for the District. I left the RCSD 1980 to serve as a High School Principal in the Parishville-Hopkinton CSD and the following year, in 1981, I was appointed by the BOE as their new Superintendent of Schools. For the following 20 years I continued serving as a Superintendent, first in the Parishville-Hopkinton CSD (1981-84), then Williamson CSD (1984-89), on to the Gouverneur CSD (1989-97), and finishing at Oswego City School District (1997-2001) before retiring. While I was in Williamson, I negotiated a contract that included support for my graduate study and received my Ph.D. in 1989. During my years with the Gouverneur CSD I enjoyed teaching in Graduate School in the Education Administration at St. Lawrence University (1990-97) where I was responsible for two graduate courses entitled, The Negotiations Process and School Law. From 1999-2001 I was an Adjunct Professor at SUNY Oswego teaching in the Superintendent Development Program and then in 2001-05 I was a full-time Visiting Professor at SUNY Oswego teaching Models of Education, Reflective Teaching Methods, Integrated Methods, and Critical Thinking about Home, School and Community. From 2005-12, I served and a Core Faculty member at the Union Institute and University in Cincinnati, OH responsible for planning, guiding, and approving Ph.D. students' work, their research, and their dissertations.

I'm still trying to learn what life's all about. I just visited a funeral home where one of my car buddies was laid out and his family had cards to hand out as you signed the Visitor's Register. On one side was a photo of Bernie in his red 1936 Ford convertible with the top down taken at full speed on the race track and on the back it read, "Life should not be a journey to the grave with the intention of arriving safely in a pretty and well preserved body, but rather to skid in broadside in a cloud of smoke, thoroughly used up, totally worn out, and loudly proclaiming, 'WOW!', what a ride!" This makes me smile just a little a bit.

I think life and living is about family, friends, love and kindness.

46

"He has told, O mortal, what is good,
and what does the LORD require of you
but to do justice, and to love kindness,
and to walk humbly with your God?"

— Micah 6:8

Good News Travels Fast

It was the summer of 1982, on a Saturday morning, while I was sitting in my office that I heard a few sounds that I faintly recognized. They were the same ones I had made when I unloaded Johnny Johnston's HD-6 Caterpillar bulldozer that I had borrowed from him for a weekend when we started construction on our cabin in Bath-Cameron. But for some reason I paid no attention. First it was the grating of steel on steel and then a loud thud as the steel ramps of the trailer slammed down on the payment. First there was one and then a few seconds later, the second. Then complete silence. I still didn't turn in my chair to look out the window. A few moments later I heard the unmistakable whirl of a large starter motor and then a diesel engine roaring to life. That got my attention quickly and as I swirled around my chair and looked out the window, there was David McKnight! David was a member of the board of education and he was on the seat of his huge dozer and he was backing it off the trailer! This entire unbelievable scenario was taking place before my very eyes right in the circular driveway and in the front of the school!

I ran out and shouted over the roar of the engine, "David, WHAT are you doing?" He smiled and shouted back, "We are not going to wait any longer and for sure as hell, we are not going to wait for Albany or the New York State Education Department's approval!" He continued, "With school opening in a few weeks and the start of the fall sports season, we are gonna fix this field NOW!" I responded and almost begging, "David we need to talk!" "Why don't you come in and have a cup of coffee?" All I got back was, "Don't have time, gotta get this done today and tomorrow, it's the only time I have!" And with that, he pushed

48

the throttle lever full forward and headed the dozer across the driveway and out behind the building toward the athletic field.

I had been in the Parishville-Hopkinton School District one year, first as the new High School Principal and for my second year, the Board of Education had appointed me as their new Superintendent of the District. During my first year, the Board conducted a search for a new super after receiving George Tyler's letter of intent to retire at the end of the school year. As a result of 86 candidates applying for the position, months spent by the Board reviewing the applications, checking references and conducting interviews, I was tagged "It" as the saying goes in the game of "Pin the Tail on the Donkey." Better stated, perhaps I was really the "donkey." I knew some of the "lay of the land" about the community, the Board members, and the staff but certainly was missing much more than appeared on the surface as I entered my new position. Evidently I really did not know the individual board members as well as I thought I did.

The majority of the Board consisted of dairy farmers and the most successful one, from my observation over the years I was there, was David McKnight. One of David's pet peeves was the District's soccer field. During my first year as the HS Principal, David had several conversations with me about the field regarding how it had poor drainage and was almost always wet. He was very familiar with this problem as one or more of his children had played soccer when they were in school. David's children had graduated before I arrived in the District. Almost as soon as I was appointed as Superintendent, David came to talk with me about what was needed to properly improve the field. He thought it needed to have drainage pipes installed underground, top soil added and the entire field re-contoured in order for it to drain properly and be dry. He wanted to know how I, as the newly appointed superintendent, could make this happen, so I outlined the procedures as I knew and understood them. I explained that the first step was that the District would need to hire an architect/engineer to make drawings, and then these plans would have to be submitted to the State Education Department for approval. If approved by the State, then funds would need to be budgeted and included in the next year's school budget. If the budget was approved by the voters, then the District would advertize for bidders and the last step in the process would be that the construction work would be awarded to the lowest bidder if all things were equal. David asked how long this process would take. I shared with him that I estimated about 2-3 months to advertize and hire an architect and have the plans developed, 3-6 months for State Education Department's approval, followed by the budget vote. The short time frame would be the following summer when school was not in session for the work to be completed. David thanked me for the information and left my office.

It was just two weeks after David's visit that on the fateful Saturday I heard the dozer's engine spring to life in the front of the school. By Sunday, the next day, all the drainage pipes had been installed in the ditches that had been dug with David's backhoe, the new top soil graded and the field seeded with help of his farm laborers and a group of community volunteers he had enlisted. At the next Board meeting all members thanked David for donating the materials and labor for improving the athletic field. When the fall sports season started that year, the new grass had had its first mowing. As we stood on the side lines at that first game, David was pleased to tell me, "So much for the State Education Department; this is the way things get done in the North Country!" And no one in Albany was ever the wiser...until now!

Also during my first year as the new superintendent, I had a visit from the Parishville Fire Chief. The Chief stopped in my office and we chatted a bit. It took awhile to get to what the visit was all about and what was on his mind. He shared with me that the Department had been raising money for several years by running a Bingo game each week. With money earned from bingo, the Department had ordered a new tanker fire truck and it was scheduled to be delivered that weekend. A parade had been planned and our school marching band would be leading the procession, with the new fire truck following them, through town. He invited me to attend the event as his guest. I assured him I would be there Saturday morning. As he was leaving he dropped the 'bomb', "Oh, one other thing, could we use the school's new portable video camera to record the parade?" I replied, "Of course, when would you like to pick it up?" This was a challenging request at the time. Video was just coming into its own and had just become available on the market. The camera and separate recorder were large, heavy, and very expensive and it was the only one the school owned.

Saturday arrived and I went to the office early to do some paper work before the parade. A few minutes prior to the starting time, I walked from the school down to the middle of town. It seemed the whole community had turned out for the arrival of the new fire fighting apparatus. As the marching band came up Main Street and across the bridge, the new truck stopped at the water's edge. The crew in their finest parade dress uniforms jumped off, put the huge supply hose from the truck into the water, revved up the engine, and began pumping a column of water high into the air. Everyone was hooting and hollering and having a grand old time. No one seemed to mind the spray in the air and getting a little wet. This continued for about 10 minutes before the marching band started the parade off again up Main Street toward the school. As the procession turned the corner of School Street things quieted down just a bit and a person in the crowd was pointing and yelling. Everyone started to look in the direction he was pointing and soon everyone was pointing to the column of smoke up in the hills. The marching firemen jumped on their new truck and headed out of town towards the source of the column of smoke that was now rising into a great cloud. The truck arrived at the location of the fire just in time to save the cellar. The entire house had burnt to the ground and all that was left were the remnants of the fire in the basement area. When the Chief returned the camera on Monday morning, I asked him if he had the whole parade on tape. He knew exactly what I was asking. We had a good laugh together and thus began my weekly invitation from him to play poker with the volunteer firemen at the fire hall.

Also that first year I had to hire a new elementary principal. Steve Black had just finished his administrative work and certification at the University of Buffalo and was seeking his first administrative position. Steve had dropped out of school at 17, joined the Marines, served with honor and completed his GED before being discharged. He immediately enrolled at the University under the GI Bill and had earned both his Bachelor's and Master's Degrees. After reviewing all applications and completing final interviews I believed he was a good match for the position and the District. It turned out he was! Steve became a high school principal and then the superintendent in the same district he moved to after leaving Parishville-Hopkinton CSD. Steve served for many years in South Glenn Falls until his retirement and currently is a professor at Florida University.

One evening, in Parishville, I received a call from Kathy, Steve's wife asking if I could come right over. I could tell there was a bit of panic in her voice. When I arrived I asked what was going on and Kathy pointed upstairs. I ran up the stairs, down the hall to the last bedroom, and there was Steve, the terrified Marine, standing on the bed with badminton racket in his hand wildly swinging at a bat that was flying around the room. The game ended with Steve 1 and the bat 0.

As the new superintendent, I had to hire a replacement for the position of HS principal. I thought the best match would be Dwayne Adsitt. Dwayne eventually moved on to a superintendent's position and served many years in two districts until he retired. Dwayne had three girls and the youngest was Connie. Charlotte had invited Connie to stay overnight. Early the next morning the area experienced a strong earthquake. I woke up and hearing a roaring noise, I ran downstairs to the cellar as I thought we had a chimney fire which does create a roar as air rushes in to supply the fire. Everything looked OK with the wood stove and I ran back upstairs trying to figure why the house was shaking and where the noise was coming from. I looked out the window and there were large waves on the water and the trees were swaying back and forth and making the weird sound. It finally dawned on me that there had been an earthquake and the aftershocks were still affecting us.

I dropped Connie off at school for her Kindergarten class that morning. The town and school were abuzz about the morning's earthquake. Taking advantage of the teachable moment, Connie's teacher asked what each child was doing that morning and were they aware and awake at the moment of the quake. Connie raised her hand and said she was awake. Her teacher asked her what she saw and heard and Connie replied, "I saw Mr. Buehler running around the house in his underwear shouting that there was a fire in the chimney."

In 1989 I was hired as the new Superintendent of Schools for the Gouverneur School District and served until 1997. During my tenure there, I was sitting in my office early one morning when the phone rang. High School Principal John Dixon was on the other end asking me if I could come to his office double time. When I arrived he told me that a student who had just gotten off one of the busses that were unloading out in front of the school and walked into the office to tell the secretary that someone had a gun on the bus. We quickly called the bus garage and requested them to radio the drivers to hold them in line and not return to the garage until they were released. We then spoke to the student to find out which bus he had ridden to school. By this time all the students were off the busses and were either in school or just entering the building. The student told us he did not know who had the gun, only that he saw a gun. John and I walked out to the line of busses and boarded the identified one. The drivers were all chatting with each other on their radios wondering why they were being held. The driver of the bus we boarded was unaware that anything was amiss on his trip. We searched the bus and a loaded .38 revolver was found tucked under the seat over the wheel well. The police arrived and were questioning the student who reported seeing the gun. We had the roster of riders and those students were brought to the office and quickly the State Police were able to identify the student who had the gun on the bus. The real hero was the young man who reported the incident.

I returned to my office, dealt with all the calls from the media, and then called Charlotte to tell her about my morning adventure. She was at work at her school in Webster. Her phone rang and when she answered I said, "Hi hon. How s your day going?" She said, "Fine and how's yours?" To which I replied, "Well we had a little excitement this morning." And she said, "I know, I had the radio on this morning on my drive to school and NPR reported a student had a loaded revolver on the school bus in the Gouverneur School District." I was astonished and answered, "NPR?" Calmly she replied, "Yeah, good news travels fast!" "You OK?" Everything OK" "John OK?" "Kids OK?" I answered everything with "Yeah." And then finally, "Love you, have a great day!"

Dr. Jim Berry was one of the District's elementary principals and I supported him when he was searching for a position in higher education. While in the Gouverneur CSD he also provided part-time coverage as the Assistant Superintendent for Curriculum and Instruction. He had been in the District several years and had served in an outstanding manner and he felt he was ready to move on to other challenges. He soon was offered a position at Eastern Michigan University in the Educational Administration Department. He had only a few months in which to sell his home and make the move. The real estate market at the time was not stellar to say the least. After a brief local listing he was in a somewhat panic mode having had no queries or interested persons. A new service was just starting to be offered by an auction company in Syracuse which was that the company would conduct all the advertizing, then come on site and hold an auction to sell both the contents and the house on a set date. Jim and his wife decided they would contract for this service. Since this was a large three story home they had, over the years, acquired numerous pieces of furniture that they would not be taking with them.

The auction date was set for a Saturday and a few days before Jim stopped by my office for a chat. "Gary, I'm a bit worried about the auction this weekend." "I'm feeling that there isn't much interest in town and we need to sell the house and this is our last opportunity to do so." "Could you do me a favor?" I replied, "Of course Jim, what do you need?" Quickly he said, "Well, if you and Charlotte aren't doing anything this weekend, we'd like you to come to the auction just so it appears that we have a larger crowd of interested bidders." "You don't have to buy anything, just come to the auction." I told Jim not to worry, I'd speak with Charlotte over dinner and we'd be there on Saturday.

During dinner Charlotte said, "Well if we are going on Saturday we better go down to the hardware store and buy a couple of lawn chairs so we'll be able to sit and be comfortable." We arrived 20 minutes before the auction with our new chairs and set them up. Jim was right; there was a very small crowd. As advertised, the firm's owner/attorney announced that they would sell the house and property first before selling the contents. Then the auctioneer began his rapid fire chatter, "OK folks, you've seen the house this morning, you walked through it with our staff, it is lovely." "The high 10' ceilings, circular staircase in the entrance foyer, the formal dining room, the large kitchen and we are selling this today with all the appliances, the formal dining room, the large front living room with fireplace, the four bedrooms on the second floor, and the finished third floor which has been used as a dance studio." "Did you notice that beautiful the hardwood floor?" "The third floor is complete with another bedroom which makes a total of five and another full bathroom on that floor." "This space could be easily converted to a separate apartment to rent if you choose or it could be an in-law apartment." "Who'll start the bidding at 135?" "135, 135, 135, do I have 125, 125, 125?" "Who'll start us out at 110, 110, 110?" "OK folks, we are all going to walk through this beautiful home together right now and we'll be back here in 15 or 20 minutes." "Follow me."

Fifteen minutes later, "OK folks, you have seen everything again." "Who'll start us off?" "Where would you like to start the bidding?" There was complete and utter silence. No one moved. No one said a word. All I was thinking was this is really bad for Jim. I was wondering how this was going to turn out. I thought to myself, this auction needs to get started so I raised my hand and blurted out, "Forty-five thousand." The auctioneer picked up the pace quickly, "I have 45, 45, looking for 50." "50, 50, who'll give me 50?' "FIFTY…fifty…who'll give me forty seven five, f o r t y-s e v en-five?" His words just hung in the air. "Going once, do I have f o r t y-s e v e n-five?" "Going twice, do I have f o r t y-s e v e n-five?" " Folks, this is a final sale today!" "Forty-seven-five, forty-seven-five." Long pause…"Sold for FORTY-FIVE!" "Come on up here to the front and sign these papers and then folks just give us a couple of minutes and we'll continue and sell all the furniture on the front lawn and everything else marked with the red tags that are still in the house." "We'll bring 'em out as we move along and sell everything."

When I heard the word SOLD I looked at Charlotte and she looked at me and I said, "What just happened?" And she said, "I think we just bought a house?" After signing the papers I slowly walked back to my chair. I glanced over at Jim and his wife and saw their sad and disappointed faces as I knew they owed the bank more than what the auction sale had netted. The auction of furnishings then commenced and

Charlotte leaned over to me and whispered, "Well now we have a house what are we going to put in it?" That day we bought the dining room table and chairs, the living room furniture, two bedroom sets, and a few other things I can't remember.

This wasn't the end of the Berry house saga. Three years later, Charlotte and I are at our other home in Pultneyville for the weekend and the phone rang on a Sunday afternoon. "Hi Gary, this is Bill." "Hi Bill, what's up?" Bill Lacy owned his own real estate company in Gouverneur and was also a teacher in the District. Bill continued, "I have this couple with me from out of state this weekend and I've shown them every house I have listed and all the multi-listings and they haven't found anything that interests them." "We were just driving back to my office and we passed your house." "They said that your place was just what they were looking for." "Would you mind if I show them inside so I can get an idea of what they like?" Knowing Bill well, I said, "The key to the back door is in the garage on the top of the electrical panel box." Two hours later Bill called back, "They love your house." "Is it for sale?" I said I'll call you back in a few minutes." I told Charlotte what transpired and we decided we could find another place if we sold this one. I called Bill back, "Yes Bill, we would consider selling." The reply from Bill was, "What do you want for it?" I guess I wasn't ready for that question, "Ah, ah, what it is assessed at." To which Bill responded, "How much is that?" "Bill, I don't remember." "OK Gary, I'll look it up and get back to you."

Bill stopped in to see me Monday morning and told me they were agreeable to the assessed value price and shared that this would be a cash deal so we could close as soon as I wanted. The couple was from Michigan of all places; that's where Jim was moving to! The new owners didn't want to drive back for the closing and wanted to know if I was agreeable to having one lawyer in Gouverneur handle the closing for the both of us. I suggested, Bob Leader, who was the School District's attorney. Bob took care of the details and one afternoon I went to his office to sign the papers. As were we sitting there I told him the story of the sale and what else I had learned from Bill. The couple who bought the house, the wife grew up in Gouverneur as a little girl and wanted to retire in three years and return to the area. Bob asked me what they were

56

going to do with the house in the interim. I told him that I didn't have a clue. I sat and looked across the desk at Bob and his big broad smile and he said, "Well, why don't I call them and ask THEM!" He did and they told him they were going to rent it for three years until they were able to retire and move to Gouverneur. Then Bob asked me what I was going to do when I moved out at the end of the month? Bob called them right back and asked them if they wanted to rent it back to me. Agreed! So in one afternoon, in less than an hour, we sold a home, signed a rental agreement and I returned back to the same bed I had gotten out of that morning. It was the easiest move we ever had.

One more story about that house. When I arrived as the new superintendent, Mike Derrigo was the High School Principal. He was an outstanding administrator, ran a tight ship, and was well respected by the community and students alike. Mike had been principal for several years and when Jim Berry took his new professorship at the University, it left an open position for the Assistant Superintendent's position. Mike Derrigo wanted a change of venue in the District and asked if I would consider him for that position. I agreed and recommended him the BOE and he was appointed. Now my task was to search and hire a new high school principal to fill the big shoes left by Mike. I found what I thought was a great replacement in the person of John Dixon. It was to be John's first principalship. He had two little kids, had just finished his Master's degree, needed his wife to continue in her position until they could sell their home and move to Gouverneur. John really wanted the position but funds for an apartment weren't in their family's budget. Remember that third floor dance studio/apartment? John was appointed the new principal and for his first year in Gouverneur, lived in the dance studio/apartment as my invited guest. Most evenings we were busy with school activities and meetings so it was rare when we both were at home at the same time. Our normal greetings when out paths did cross sort of went like this, "John, how was your day?" And he would reply, "Not too bad except for that damned PITA I work for, he is so unreasonable, and how was your day?" To which I'd reply something like, "I had a great day except for that blockhead that runs the high school." That was the end of "school talk" evening.

Post script: Dr. Steven Black received his Ed.D. degree from Syracuse University while serving as High School Principal at the South Glenn Falls School District. Dr. Jim Berry still holds his position as Head of the Department of Education at Eastern Michigan University; John Dixon served the Gouverneur School District in an outstanding manner until his retirement and remains a respected member of that community. Mike Derrigo worked as the Assistant Superintendent for three years and decided he wanted to apply for a superintendency. He asked me if I would support his effort which of course I did. He was successful and secured a position before the year's end. He retired from that same position after many years of success in leading that District. These are just a few of the hundreds of smiles along the way with good friends and professional colleagues.

The Amazing Charlotte

I confess the title of this chapter is not my doing; the culprits responsible are Joani, Rae-Ellen, and Melanie. They are the members of a writing group that were already organized and had interacted with each other before Joani invited me to join them in their monthly sessions. The first hundred pages of this, what was originally thought to be novella of my summers at Uncle George's and Aunt Erma's farm, were tossed in the file drawer. I knew I had to begin anew to tell 'my story.' When I thought all was lost, the above mentioned three musketeers rode in and my 'day' was saved. I was invited to join a group of experienced authors and ushered into the inner sanctum of an experienced troupe of writers. I have benefitted from their sage counsel, insightful comments and suggested changes and, most importantly, their interest and support in assisting me in telling my story.

This memoir cannot be solely about me; it can only be about us. As this story telling journey unfolds and the words find their way to the printed page, 'my' story really becomes 'our' story, that is, the tale of the two of us. Charlotte and I have been together almost four times longer than we, as children growing up, lived at home with our parents, or in my case, with my grandparents. I think about what my grandparents taught or tried to teach me in those years they spent with me, and now I think about what Charlotte has taught me having the patience of being with me for such an expanded amount of time and I realize that our time together is growing shorter. Thus this chapter with its convincing title is the result of the musketeers' suggestion. They told me I had to develop it and use their title. Thanks guys for the guidance and thank YOU

Charlotte for YOU and all you have done and as the good book states, for having the patience of Job.

The 1960's and '70's were interesting decades. Charlotte and I, as both individuals, as a couple, and as well as a family, experienced and were an integral part of those decades of change. They were exciting years as well as difficult in terms of the impact of change that it had on our country and society in general. We not only faced and embraced change but somehow we all managed to pass through the decades unscathed (I think) to the other side. Some were not so lucky especially those who served in Vietnam. On an otherwise insignificant and unmarked day on the calendar in the Year of our Lord 1974, one of those exciting as well as difficult changes was experienced on a very personal level. I think I remember Charlotte meeting me at the front door after school one day and although these may have not been the exact words uttered, they are the ones I think I remember... "I'm tired of cooking, baking, and cleaning, I want something more. I want to go to college and I want a career but I'm too old." And I replied something like this, "Hon, how old are you now?" "Thirty-two!" was the answer. And I responded back, "Well how old will you be next year if you don't go to college?" I felt a cold wind blow in from the north that day. The next day when I arrived home Charlotte told me about the College Level Educational Program (CLEP) exam honored by SUNY Brockport which allows one to receive college credit if they successfully test for and pass various subject area exams included in the CLEP. Charlotte signed up for and took the exam and received enough total credits to enroll as a full time student at the sophomore level at SUNY Brockport. In three years she graduated with a BS and with the honor of Summa Cum Laude. She then decided to attend Alfred University on a full time basis for her Master's Degree. In just two years she graduated with highest honors and with a 60-hour Master's Degree in School Psychology. Yes, the Amazing Charlotte!

While at Alfred, she arranged her classes to be scheduled from Monday through Wednesday. She would leave home for Alfred University on Sunday evenings where she stayed in a motel evenings until returning home after her classes were finished late Wednesday. At this time our kids were 16, 14, and 8 years old. During her away time, I played house Mom and Dad for and with the three of them. We all had a satisfying time together and many stories to tell the real Mom when she returned home from Alfred each week. Oh, the stories that were told! One was the pickle juice story, and yes, I can now admit the pickle juice story the kids told Mom was true. Once, and only once, I swear, did I put pickle juice in the hamburgers! Why? Just because! The 'baked tomato-cheese-bread thingy' wasn't the greatest dish known to mankind, but when you're hungry, you ate it. Hot dogs were a staple—whether they were fried or baked, or combined with beans, cheese, macaroni or all three. Real meat treat day was fried hamburger patties (with or without cheese) accompanied by baked or fried potatoes. And the best of all, baked bread rolls with a hot dog stuffed in the middle. Jell-O was the standard dessert followed by an evening snack of; Charlie's chips and/or pretzels, or Twinkies, or Oreos and when the cupboard was bare, good old fashion stand by, popcorn with way too much melted butter. The time with the kids was very special for me.

Somehow we all were able to get off to school on time in the mornings. We managed to take care of preparing dinner, doing the dishes, and doing some light housekeeping after school each week day when Mom was out of town. We spent our evenings together with the girls doing their home work and with me correcting my students' papers and planning class lessons. Then all of us would watch some TV, have a snack or make popcorn and then off to bed. Good times were had by all (I think?). One time we all were caught short and our housekeeping secrets were revealed. It made sense to me (and the kids with a little convincing) to try to have the house in perfect order when Mom returned home late on Wednesday but not to worry about it until Wednesday afternoon. Why waste effort making beds, washing dishes, vacuuming, picking up dirty clothes and towels on Monday and Tuesday when it all could be done at once and only once after school on Wednesday? It's just a waste of time and besides, if you did it every day, you would have to do it on Wednesday all over again. Just do it once and do a good job and you are done and no one is the wiser. Well that theory worked extremely well in practice until one day when Mom came home early, much earlier than expected. There was a flurry of activity that afternoon! At least that's the way I remember it! We were busted! Better check this out with Charlotte, Tonja, Tammy, and Todd... After Charlotte's graduation we were a two career family and I am still so proud of her and all of her accomplishments. She was a much better student than I was and don't tell a soul, she is a heck of a lot smarter also! Remember the story of when Charlotte attended the math class for me at Roberts Wesleyan and took notes so I could do the class assignments and take the exams without ever stepping a foot inside of the class room? She also took a music appreciation course for me abiding by the same stipulations set by the math professor. As a part of the course she had to attend concerts at the Eastman School of Music and the Rochester Philharmonic practices. And I successfully completed the course without taking a single note only because Charlotte covered all the classes and field trips. Yes...THE amazing Charlotte!

I have had an interest in automobiles all of my life and I have participated in various aspects of the automobile hobby. One segment of the hobby is drag racing. In 1963 I bought a new Ford which was basically designed to be a race car, if ordered with all the critical options. It was a 427 cu. in., 425 horse power engine, two-four barrel carburetors, a 4-speed manual shift transmission, 4:88 Equal lock rear. It was built for the drag strip, not for the highway. Yes, the amazing Charlotte competed in drag racing at the Savannah drag strip with this car, winning a trophy. This was at a time when it was extremely rare for a woman to drive and race a drag car! I think it became a drag car on the street on grocery shopping days as the oil was usually down a bit from normal levels and I know rear tires had to be replaced frequently.

In the 1990's I became interested in motorcycles and bought a new Harley Davidson Classic motorcycle. This was a large bike built for two riders. After I 'dumped' us on the ground one time, Charlotte informed me that, "If you are going to continue to ride motorcycles, I don't trust you any more, I don't like not being in control, and I'll only ride if I have my own bike." We quickly became a two Harley Davidson motorcycle family. Charlotte now had her own Harley. My bucket list contained a visit to the annual gathering of Harleys at Sturgis, South Dakota. This is a town of 5,000 that grows to 700,000 Harley participants for one week a year. We attended the event and following the Sturgis Rally, spent several days in Yellowstone National Park riding our bikes. We also rode through the Painted Desert National Park. What glorious open air riding experiences! Incredible! And what a great sport Charlotte was on that adventure. And, as expected, Charlotte would only ride her Harley after she took the Safe Rider Course which, of course, I did not.

Speaking of being a good sport and bucket lists…I had on my bucket list to drive a hot rod to California and back and we accomplished that just two years ago. I have an 'Old School' hot rod, a 1930 Ford Model A sedan. 'Old School' translates to the way cars were equipped 'back in the day.' That is: no air conditioning, power brakes, automatic transmission, power windows, power steering, radio, basically, no nothing. Driving across the Mojave Desert during the day with temps always in the 100's, it gets mighty warm! And that's my Charlotte, "Count me in!"

In the early days of our marriage, with two girls, and then a boy, a new home and all on a teacher's salary, there wasn't a lot of money to go around. Charlotte created, made, and sewed most of the girl's clothes and dresses and even made a sports jacket for me to wear to school. She was a frugal shopper. She had to be. I was mechanically inclined so we drove old used cars that I worked on to keep them on the road. One day she found a picnic table that a store had on sale that needed repair and it was in the garage when I arrived home. That table moved with us for 30 years! It served as a saw table when we built our cabin and then became our kitchen table there. It followed us to Parishville, Gouverneur, and even to Oswego where it was transformed into a rainbow of colors but always retained the saw cuts on the benches from the various construction projects where it had served double duty.

Among the long list of used "almost junk" cars we drove, there was an old 1960's something VW beetle. I bought it from Jerry Bauman for $50 when he could no longer drive it because the front end was 'frozen', that is, seized up and would not move. I repaired it and it was our car for awhile. Charlotte bought a new bicycle for me and had help from the store employee somehow getting it inside the VW in the back seat but couldn't get it out of the car by herself when she returned home. My present was all wrapped and waiting for me in the driveway when I returned home from school that day. There in the driveway was our ancient VW, completely wrapped up and totally covered in newspaper comics with a big red ribbon wrapped around it from the top to bottom of the car with the huge red bow on the roof. Marvelous creativity!

Postscript: As I write this I am sitting in a cabin at Elk Lake looking out at the mountains of the Dix range in the Adirondacks. Charlotte left very early this morning wearing her favorite hiking/climbing baseball cap with the words, "The Mountains are calling." Yes indeed, they are! Sometime after her seventieth birthday she told me she wanted to become a 46er, that is, to climb all 46 of the high peaks in the Adirondacks. Today marks her 26th! I can't hike the way she does. Today will be a 15 mile or so round trip. I have tried and have hiked one of the easy and fairly flat trails part way until the steep part began and that was only a 9 miles round trip. "You go girl!" She has hiked various peaks with her daughter, each of our grandchildren at different times, and also with many friends, and professional guides. What wonderful memories she has made for our children and grandchildren. All of her hikes have been recorded, photographed, and shared with a representative of the ADK. What a love!

Yes, the amazing Charlotte!

Updated Postscript: I wrote the first draft of this chapter on Thursday, June 23, 2016. We returned home the next day on Friday. Then on Saturday our writing group received an email from Joani reminding us that we would meet at her home the following Tuesday at noon. Her email was sent at 11:16 am Saturday morning. Less than 12 hours later she had a massive heart attack at the family's lake cottage and left our world for someplace else. I'll never know what her last story was that she wrote but I do know the world lost a bright light and a most loving and kind person. Joani, Bob, Charlotte Kay and I have been close friends for fifty years. Oh for the mysteries of life we struggle with and try to make sense out of them while trying to fathom how the end of our own story will be written.

Let Me Tell You about Eugene

I bought my first .22 rifle when I was 14 with money that I had saved and with my grandmother's blessing. I still have that gun today. When I was 16 and in high school, I thought that it would be a good idea to go with a pal of mine and to do some target shooting. As most 16-year-olds are apt to do, this hair brain scheme of an idea was not well thought out nor well planned. I met George after school at his house and we drove out to Greece to my home, picked up my rifle, and decided to drive around to find a place to shoot at targets. Speaking of hair brained, we did not have any paper targets but we did have cans of soda which we were about to consume after we stopped at a store for snacks we planned to use the empty cans for targets. We knew we had to get out of the city to shoot so we started driving along the Lake Ontario Parkway looking for a place to set up the cans off the highway and shoot at them. It was cold and the ground was snow-covered and as we drove along we noticed a many ducks and geese along the lake shore. What better challenge could one find than to roll down the window of the car (remember it was cold and in the winter) to try to hit one of these birds? Do it the easy way, right? Just one shot and they all scattered and we missed the target. As we drove further along we noticed that the water fowl were in the median of the highway but every time we stopped the car and got out to shoot at them, they would fly off. Now we were challenged! So I came up with what I thought was a brilliant plan. I would lie on the hood of the car with my feet against the windshield and the toes of my shoes behind the rear edge of the hood so as not to slide off when we slowed down or stopped. We proceeded slowly down the highway while taking careful aim to try to hit one of these 'targets'. We

65

were so intent in shooting a water fowl we failed to notice a car on the opposite side of the highway until it was too late. Soon we found ourselves in the back seat of the Greece police car. George's car was towed away and we were given a proper tongue lashing with a detailed description of what we could be arrested for, along with a heavy fine and jail time. We sat in silence as we were driven to Greece Police Headquarters. Upon arriving we were taken inside and placed in separate rooms. After what seemed like eons of time, we were escorted back to the police cruiser and placed in the back seat once again.

Neither George nor I had any idea where we were being taken. Since my home was closer to police headquarters than George's, I was driven to my home first. It soon became apparent that phone calls were made from the station while we were in the separated rooms. When we arrived at my home, my grandmother was there to greet us as the officer explained what he had caught us doing and that I could have been taken to jail but instead he was taking me home for my parents to deal with me and he was confiscating my gun. He then left to take George home to his parents. I cannot begin to imagine what was going through my grandmother's mind or how she felt about what I had done, but I do remember that she sat down to talk with me. Part of that conversation was a question and answer session regarding my knowledge of right from wrong, the difference between proper target shooting and how to use a gun as opposed to what I had been caught doing and what were my thoughts about responsible gun ownership and my actions.

A week later my grandmother took me to the police station and had me explain that I understood proper gun ownership as well as the responsibility for owning a gun and using it properly and safely. I apologized to the police officer for what I had done. The police returned the rifle to my grandmother for her safe keeping. After an extended period of time she allowed me to keep the rifle in my room until such time that I could demonstrate that I could be a responsible gun owner. There was never another problem with that rifle.

I did not know all the unspoken family secrets about Eugene when George and I went 'target' shooting. As a youngster growing up, I heard the name Eugene mentioned just once when I was looking through a box of old family photos. Someone, I don't remember who, commented to another adult in the room, "Here's a picture of Eugene!"

Being an inquisitive little guy, I naturally asked "Who's Eugene?"

I could tell by the response that there were many intense feelings and emotions associated with my question and conceivably even some embarrassment. That was the one and only time as a youngster that I heard Eugene's name mentioned.

Until I was 11 years old and in the sixth grade I thought my family consisted of my mother, father and brother Paul. It was then I learned that my parents were truly my grandparents and I had been adopted by them. Much later I became aware that my grandparents had five children, and in birth order they were: Eugene, Emma, Erma, Fritz, and Paul. Through the adoption process, they legally became my brothers and sisters. On the family tree, Emma was my birth mother and Erma was her sister. Eugene, Fritz, and Paul were my mother's brothers. In the final analysis, through birth, Eugene was my uncle, and through the adoption process he legally became another one of my siblings as did Emma, Erma, Fritz, and Paul.

Until the accidental occurrence of finding the picture of Eugene in a box of family photos, in my mind and in reality, he did not exist as a part of our family. Many years later I asked my uncle/brother Paul if he knew about Eugene, who he was, and what happened to him? To try to put his answer into perspective, Paul was only three years old at the time of the episode involving Eugene so perhaps what Paul shared with me was what he had been told as a youngster growing up. What I do remember Paul revealing to me through all my questioning was that Eugene was his oldest brother and that he was no longer alive. In pursuing the matter with question after question, he told me that his brother Eugene was caught stealing 5 gallon cans of gas from the gas depot in the neighborhood to resell.

As part of his explanation, he said the family did not have a lot of money as it was during the Depression and it was a tough time in which to grow up. He also told me that after Eugene was apprehended by the police and charged, he was sent to reform school. Naturally, I asked him what happened after that. Paul told me that Eugene was in a Police paddy wagon being transferred and moved suddenly and a police officer shot him. Naturally I asked a zillion more questions and Paul said that he did not know any more of what had happened other than what he already told me.

I've thought about this narrative ever since I had that difficult conversation with Paul so very many years ago. As a matter of fact, I have thought about it almost my entire life in the same way that I was curious and wondered about the story of my family, parents, grandparents, mother and birth father. After I retired from my career I decided that I wanted to try to find out more about my uncle/brother Eugene, his life, his story, and his journey and what really happened to him. Based on the very sketchy information that uncle/brother Paul had shared with me I was driven to try to figure out what really had happened so many years ago and why all the secrecy surrounding the very mention of his name. In retrospect the thought that now comes to my mind is…if you don't want to know the answer, don't ask the question. I was willing to ask. For me it had all the intrigue of a murky and shrouded mystery and I wanted to solve it just to satisfy myself.

I started my search for the answers with a series of U.S. Census reports focused on the Buehler name and the known resident address at 1519 Emerson Street. I was able to narrow down a period of time when Eugene's name, as a member of the Buehler family residing at 1519 Emerson Street, appeared on the census roll and then on the next census report the name was not there. Since the US censes is taken every 10 years the search was now narrowed to a decade, the 1930's. I also tried several computer searches and spent time trying to uncover any little tidbit of information about Eugene Buehler who resided on Emerson Street in Rochester, New York. Luckily I did find a search reference footnote regarding the name related to a court case and a new State law that had just been enacted which referenced the year 1935 but other than the year, no specific date or other information was listed. With only this one little piece of information I went to the Rundle Library and began searching the archives of the *Rochester Democrat and Chronicle* (D&C) and the *Times Union* (TU) newspapers beginning with January 1, 1935 hoping to find a clue or some other reference to Eugene in one of the papers. After reading all the headlines of every story in each section of every daily edition recorded on microfiche, I found the answer.

There it was in large block print headlines on the screen of the microfiche reader and it literally jumped off the screen from the page of the March 3,1935 edition of the D&C;

Two Youths Held After Gunfights — Bullets Fly as
Police Pursue Pair in a Mad Flight; One Shot in Leg;
Car is Wrecked; Holdups in Rochester Laid to 2
Jailed in Syracuse.

I could not believe what I was reading: *"Captured after surviving gunfire several times in the seven hour chase two Rochesterians, one wounded, were held last night by Syracuse police. Four times yesterday morning they ran the gauntlet of rifle and revolver fire in a wild pursuit through Central New York until their car crashed into an abutment and they surrendered. Eugene Buehler, 21, of 1519 Emerson St., was shot in the right leg by a rifle bullet that pierced the car's body."*

As I read further I was astonished and realized that there was much more to the story than Paul had told me or perhaps that he did not even know. The article went on to explain how shots were exchanged between a State Trooper and the two men in the car with one of the bullets going through the Trooper's hat. I thought this is was material that movies are made about which does not happen in real life. But there it was, a tale of intrigue outlining that the two gunmen in the automobile exchanged fire with New York State Troopers with bullets going through the windshield and the radiator of the police car and the gunmen escaped the roadblock that the State Police had set up.

As I read further it became more unbelievable even in my mind's eye as the article outlined that the chase proceeded to Syracuse and the Syracuse Police Department's Machine Gun Squad had been sent to the suburbs of the city. Once again the police were eluded and the car sped by at 80 miles an hour, stopped, turned around and was now headed toward Skaneateles. At yet another roadblock that had been set up, gunfire was exchanged once again and one of the men in the automobile was wounded.

That person was Eugene. After the gun battle, their car crashed into an abutment and two State Troopers approached the car to make arrests. Eugene was taken to St. Joseph hospital for treatment from the bullet wound from the rifle and was placed under police guard. At the hospital Eugene and the other man in the car did not give police their real names. After an ongoing investigation Eugene and the other person apprehended in the car crash were identified as having been charged for holdups in Rochester after being paroled from Elmira Reformatory.

I felt nauseous as I finished the article realizing that this was not just a story in a newspaper about criminals, robberies, a police chase, but a story that had a direct connection with me and my family. I was left wondering why? How could this have happened? What went wrong? I realized that it was no wonder we never talked about Eugene all the time I was growing up. Then it came flooding back to me, the day that I looked at the photograph and the person with me exclaimed, "That's a picture of Eugene" and as soon as that was said I started asking questions as an 11-year-old. I now realized why I could feel the stress and tension along with a sense of embarrassment in the room. But what I had just read did not match what Paul had told me about Eugene being shot by police in a paddy wagon. I wanted to know what else happened to Eugene. What was the rest of his story since the article said he had been shot in the leg and taken to the hospital? Did he die from the rifle bullet in the leg?

As I continued to search the archives I was going through reel after reel of microfiche films and once again the headlines in the Democrat and Chronicle leapt off the page. There it was on the screen in black and white in the June 18, 1935 issue of the D&C., three months I after I found the first article, I discovered another newspaper headline:

Felons Battle Guards in Bus, One Shot; Pilot Leader
Wounded as Five Others leap at Deputies;
Prisoners from Attica Yield as Rochester Gunman Drops

Again that sick and empty feeling in the pit of my stomach returned as I read about the event that happen on a bus in East Bloomfield. In

1935 there was a new ruling by the State Attorney's Office that convicted felons that had used a firearm during the commission of their crime would receive additional sentencing on gun carrying charges. There were a number of convicted felons who were being transported from Attica State prison to Syracuse to appear before a judge for additional sentencing as a result of the State Attorney's new ruling. Eugene was on that bus that was in the convoy headed to Syracuse. The article was full of details explaining how four armed guards on the bus were overpowered by the men as the bus driver pulled over to the shoulder of the road on State Route 5 in heavy traffic.

The D&C commentary explained that when the attack on the guards occurred on the bus, the prisoners who had been talking suddenly became silent. A few moments before the prisoners leapt from their seats to attack the Deputies, Eugene lowered his head, and closed his eyes as an apparent prearranged signal which resulted in a furious battle inside the bus. According to the Deputies, Eugene leapt from his seat, grabbed a Deputy's gun who was sitting across the aisle on the opposite seat. There were two Deputies seated on the back seat at the rear of the bus with sawed off shotguns. The convicts were in handcuffs and as the struggle took place the Deputies in the rear of the bus with the shotguns were unable to fire for fear of hitting the other two Deputies that were involved in the fight. One of the Deputies hit Eugene and he fell forward toward the driver's seat at which point the Deputy fired four shots, two of which struck Eugene in his back. Eugene was taken to Canandaigua hospital.

In a follow-up D&C newspaper article covering the inquest at the County Courthouse in Canandaigua, the reporter wrote that in the Deputy's testimony about Buehler that even at the hospital where he was badly wounded, he winked and said to the Deputy, "I tried it, anyway." That same edition of the D&C carried a photo of Eugene in his hospital bed where he lay dying of the two bullet wounds in his back. I do know that he was in his bed in the Canandaigua Hospital for a full week before he passed away. His mother, my grandmother, was at his bedside day and night. I now understand why no one in the family ever spoke of Eugene when I was growing up and I cannot begin to imagine the pain,

71

hurt, suffering and perhaps even the guilt my grandparents felt but never talked about in my presence and kept all of this from me. I now am beginning to understand so much more about all my family members, their relationships, how and where we lived and how I was raised.

I also try to ponder what went through grandma's mind that day when she received the phone call from Greece police headquarters and later when the police car pulled into her driveway with me in the back seat. She must have had flashbacks about her oldest son, Eugene.

Record Book

U ncle Fritz was like many of us. He was a complex individual having both a bright and dark side. I was on a mission at his request as I crested the steep Gulf hill on Route 10 out of Bath and on the left I saw the pine trees that he had planted many years before. Behind the trees and well hidden was his cabin. Memories came flooding back as I remember when there was an old abandoned two story farm house on the rise exactly where the cabin still stands today. Although I was told never to go inside the abandoned house, as a 10 year old vacationing on Aunt Erma and Uncle George's farm, the empty structure was hauntingly calling me to explore it which of course I did many times. Years later, when I was in my late teens, Uncle Fritz bought this piece of land with the old house on it, removed the second floor of the structure and used the lumber to build a hunting cabin on the original stone cellar foundation. It was a very cozy place with a homey atmosphere, neat, orderly, and well appointed for a cabin. I drove around the long driveway that went by the fence on the property lines and behind the cabin and stopped at the garage. I was focused and on my mission and wondering what I might find. I located the key to the side door of the garage exactly where Fritz had told he had hidden it, I removed the pad lock, and opened the door to the musty building with the earthen floor.

Upon entering I saw the 1947 GMC truck that he had painted a deep forest green so many years ago after buying it at a farm auction. It was not a large garage and the truck filled up almost all the floor space. As I looked around, I observed the organization and neatness of this place that represented the almost compulsive nature of holding on to what was

73

his. Behind every tool hanging on the wall was, perfectly painted in red, an outline of that tool. With one quick glance anyone could tell if a tool was missing or out of place. Every hand tool including shovels, rakes, pick axes, hand axes and all the wrenches, saws, hammers, and brushes were painted with a perfect quarter of an inch of red line around the tip of each of their handles. The red stripe on every tool let you know you were holding one from Fritz's garage in your hand. There was no way in hell anyone could take or borrow a tool and not know where to return it or where it came from. This was a perfect neat and orderly garage with everything in its place and nothing was missing!

Fritz, like most of us, was a complicated person with many sides to his personality. I was 20 years old when I asked Fritz's permission to use the cabin with some of my friends for a few days during deer hunting season. It was a warm weekend and not very good weather for hunting, so for the use of the cabin I thought that, since the trim on the cabin was fading and peeling in a few spots, it would be a thoughtful gesture to scrape and paint and have it looking good for the next time Fritz was back east for a visit. The four of us in our hunting party made short work of the task and had it looking great, or so I thought, with a new coat of green paint over the old green. Months later when Fritz returned to the area he was livid about what he referred to as the careless and sloppy paint job we had done. As I thought about that hunting trip and painting the trim so many years ago I was uneasy standing in his garage looking at the red outlines of the tools and the perfect quarter inch red stripe on each handle. I finally understood why Fritz thought it was a "careless and sloppy paint job."

A step ladder was hanging on the wall and I took it down and set it up it so I could climb up to reach the rafters. Decades of dust, dirt, and grime covered the child's bike, sled, baby highchair, scooter, and metal toy truck, the boxes Fritz told me I would find were under these items. I pulled each one down and piled them in the bed of the truck along with the boxes. It was in the third box I opened that I found the item Fritz told me to take out and put in the trash barrel and burn.

One of my mother's brothers was Fritz with whom I was fascinated as a youngster growing up. He was handsome, muscular and he always had mustache, the very thin perfectly trimmed pencil type. He served in the U.S. Navy during World War II and when the war ended he moved to Seattle, Washington. He completed boot camp having just turned 20 when he married his sweetheart, Emma. As soon as he was discharged at the end of the war they moved to Settle, Washington and he embarked on designing and building a self-contained motor home. His creativity, mechanical skills and ability impressed and influenced me as a teenager. In the vernacular of the day, everyone referred to his motor home as a "house car." Today we would call it an RV. Fritz designed and built his on a large school bus/truck chassis. It was constructed utilizing an aluminum frame and outer skin of aluminum, the same construction methods and materials used today by manufactures to build RVs. It was also as modern as today's RVs complete with a kitchen stove, refrigerator, hot and cold water, furnace, self-contained bathroom with shower, holding tanks, and a double bed in the back bedroom. It was light years ahead of anything available to the general public in travel and camping trailers of this time period of 1940's. No commercial self-contained powered campers or RVs were being built at that time. When it was completed Fritz and Emma traveled the West Coast from the Washington down to Mexico City From there their travels took them across the southern states to Florida and up the East Coast to New York. I remember the night that they arrived at our home as I was awakened from a sound sleep by my grandmother to greet them since all of us had not seen them for several years. In the morning I was given a tour of their traveling "house car" and was awed by the interior and the motorcycle that was carried inside of the vehicle for use when they were parked for the evening. It was so different from what anyone else had ever seen in terms of traveling in self-contained comfort and cutting-edge technology for that era.

Every time I heard the story of his new 1947 Ford convertible as a kid I was excited. He and his wife traveled to Pennsylvania to visit some of his cousins. While there they attended a barn dance and raffle tickets were being sold as a fundraiser. Fritz did not believe in gambling and he was not involved in it while he was in the Navy. As a matter of fact he acted as the" banker" aboard his ship loaning money to shipmates who had lost it while gambling. He was reluctant to even buy a raffle ticket for a good cause. The tickets were selling for a dollar and I would guess he bought one to be social. With that one dollar investment he won a brand-new 1947 Ford convertible! Returning from Pennsylvania and pulling into our driveway, I was once again awakened so as to be a part of the celebration. I was 7 years old and I am sure that '47 Ford convertible is probably the reason I still love fast and flashy cars.

He parked his "house car" behind our home on Emerson Street and this is where he lived for a short period while he was pursuing his other entrepreneurial ideas and adventures. He purchased land on Scottsville Road and built a new Texaco gas station which he operated for short period of time. He then bought land in Spencerport and built a beautiful new home. He and his family lived there for a few years before the entrepreneurial spirit took over once again and he sold both his gas station and home to go in partnership with one of his cousins. He moved his family to Orcus Island in Puget Sound, Washington where they operated a lumber yard and hardwood store. He designed and built another home, developed a park, sold his business and retired on the Island after their boys graduated from high school. He never moved his family into the new home and it stood empty until he died. There were many sides to Fritz and it was not always an idyllic family situation for their three boys growing up or for his spouse, Emma. There were many reasons for this no doubt and I believe the major one was the war experience which he never really talked about.

He was a great hunter and fisherman and as a youngster, when we visited him on the Island, he always took us deep-sea fishing. He enjoyed deer hunting in the southern tier of New York State so much that he built the hunting cabin and, even though his residence was in Washington State, he would travel back to New York State on a regular basis for hunting season and to visit family and friends. When he was in his late 60's I learned that he was terminally ill and I flew out to Orcus Island to spend time with him. I decided that I wanted to do that rather than wait and attend his funeral. I had a good week with him and Emma and toward the end of my visit I asked him if there was anything that he wanted me to do for him. We were alone and he did tell me there was something he would like me to do. He asked that when I returned to Rochester to go to his cabin and retrieve a box of items that he had stowed away which were out of sight and hidden in the rafters of the garage at the cabin. He said that I would find some items that he had put away that were his boys' when they were young and growing up and to make sure they got them. He also said that I would find a book of records of torpedo tests that he had conducted when he was in the Navy and stationed in Newport, Rhode Island. He also mentioned in passing that he was an instructor for submarine crews and the book contained his notes for the classes that he taught and that I should just throw it in the burn barrel and get rid of it. It was just trash. I told him that I would take care of it. The next day we said our final 'goodbyes' and it was just a few weeks later that he passed away. I did not return to the Island to attend his funeral and I was comforted knowing that we spent time together just a few weeks earlier.

Fritz entered boot camp in February of 1943 and upon completion, spent a year as a torpedo instructor at the Navy base in Newport, Rode Island. He was then assigned to the USS Dortch which was newly build and commissioned by the Navy in 1943. The ship he served on was classified as a destroyer which had the responsibility for escorting large aircraft carriers. His assignment was to man and fire the ship's torpedoes. His ship and crew were involved in the capture and occupation of Saipan, the Battle of the Philippine Sea, the invasion of the Philippines, the battle of Leyte Gulf, the assault landings on Iwo Jima, Okinawa, Wake Island, and then on to Tokyo Bay, Japan. These engagements in WWII in the Pacific were some of the most difficult battles and encounters with the Japanese during the war.

When I retrieved the boxes from the rafters of the garage I found the worn hardcover copy of the book in one of the boxes that Fritz had told me about. On the cover of the book, in his handwriting, I read, "Torpedo tests, Record, Fritz Buehler, 1943, Newport, Rhode Island." I thumbed through several pages, 71 to be exact, and all these included detailed handwritten recordings of such things as; air releasing mechanism test, main engine test, warhead fiction test, assembly test, gear ratio of torpedo and service, firing test, and depth charges. Then I read page 73 and my heart was pounding as I thumbed through to the end of the book to page 199. I realized that in my hands I was holding his day-to- day journal for the entire time that he served aboard the USS Dortch. He had packed this up and hidden it away for reasons that I will never know. It could have been the nightmares, the bad memories, or even fear of a court-martial because of the detailed information it contained which included a listing of Japanese casualties, the names of US sailors lost, the names of American and Japanese ships that were sunk, the names of all the US ships in the various formations at different times including battleships, carriers, and the names and dates of every strike and engage-ment of the USS Dortch.

Following are just a few of the hundreds of entries from his journal in his own words. I share these with you to try to give you some idea what it must have been like for him aboard this battleship day in and day out, the tension, stress, fears, good and bad moments, but most importantly, his very thoughts in his own words and in his own hand...

September 22, 1944 — We (Dortch) picked up two airmen who had just crashed. At dusk we were heading away from the Philippines when our lookout reported a life raft off our starboard beam. We picked the men up — they had been on the raft for 11 days! They were quite weak!

October 12 — Our planes are attacking Formosa, but we have run into a hornets' nest, planes have been attacking us all day and night. A Jap torpedo plane put a fish into the US S Canberra; she is stopped in the water. I don't know how many killed! About 4:30, the 15th GQ ran to my battle station the sky was filled with planes, coming in low. Four Jap torpedo planes coming in low. Our five 40 inch was all around him, but couldn't get a hit, just then a plane headed for cruiser Reno (which is throwing all it had at the plane) she accounts for six planes. The plane was hit 50 or 60 yards from the Reno but instead of crashing in the water the Jap dove on the cruiser's fantail. A column of fire shot up and I could almost feel the heat. Meanwhile a plane crossed our fantail; it let its fish go in the general direction of the Lexington but missed (thank God!). The same plane came across from port to star board, we hit it and the yell went up, "We got it." The task force got 37 planes!

October 18 — I heard radio Tokyo today — they made the most exaggerated claims I've ever heard. They said they sank 53 of our ships (actually they didn't sink any). They say they shot down 1000 planes (perhaps shot down 60 since the strike began a week and a half ago). Boy! Can they bull _ _ _ _!

October 25 — This morning at 3 o'clock we went to GQ. It's pitch dark — Jap Task Force is said to be 40 miles away. (I didn't forget how to pray) ... I sure feel better now that that part is over with. I was rather uncomfortable when the 11 inch shells started exploding up off our port bow and we only had 5 inch to fire back. Thank God! For seeing us through.

November 5 — about 1 PM the bong bong of GQ sounded — we all ran to our battle stations. Bogeys were coming in. About 1:05 PM we open fired 40 mm and 20 mm. The plane swerved around and dove into the Lexington. He made no attempt whatever to pull out of his dive (suicide pilot). He hit just forward of the signal bridge in a burst of flame. Killing 16 and burning about 30. A second plane dove on the Santa Fe — she swerved and the plane crashed into the water. Two more were shot down in flames off our port beam. Went to GQ again but one of our night fighters got the plane out 18 miles!

November 6 — We pulled away from the Task Force 30 miles to rescue two airmen, pilot and gunner. Radioman was killed over the target (Manila)! We rejoin the task group at 1:30 PM. At 4:30 PM we again dropped out of formation to pick up a fighter pilot from the USS Essex - who had run out a gas! We rejoin at 5:30 PM. It is now 8:30 PM we are pulling away from Luzon. Scuttlebutt has it we attack Japan soon!! The Jap radio just made claims of sinking four of our carriers — one by submarine and three by planes — some bunk!!

November 8 — What a day — we hit another hurricane. The Dortch is bucking like a bronco. All groups in the area are waiting out the storm at sea. The Executive Officer of the Healy went over board last night. Two cans dropped back but failed to find him! We sustained some damage from the storm.

November 20 — Went to GQ at 6:00 AM. A tanker blew sky high about 1,500 yards off our port bow. I can feel the depth charges going off the whole ship shakes. Three subs snuck in and sunk the tanker with torpedoes. The tanker that was torpedoed was the Mississewa. Only 12 men out of 120 were rescued. We sank three subs — they were two-man suicide subs. All in all we dropped about 500 depth charges in the harbor today. It sure seemed odd — as the Mississewa was a tanker we refueled from on the 17th.

November 22 — Thanksgiving Day — my second in the Navy. We sure had a swell meal — Turkey and all the trimmings to go with it. The XO announced this p.m. that after refueling we were going to make a one-day strike on central Luzon on the 25th. A Jap cruiser is damaged west of Manila — we are going after it.

November 25 — Today just after the Zero attack we spotted something in the water. Looked like a mine but apparently it wasn't. We bounced about 20 shells off it did not explode. We then by this time had fallen back out of the task force. The radar on the wagons couldn't pick us up and they tried to radio us but couldn't pick us up. They reported us as sunk!!! to the task group. Egad!!!!! (No! We are still here).

December 3 — Went to church at 10:30 AM. Took communion. Sermon was on, "Prepare the Way." Had chicken for chow this noon — (didn't get enough to feed a sparrow). Made several trips over to the tanker to get torpedo stores. Also had my taste of ice cream today, first in a long time (from tender Dixie).

December 4 — Just heard that the cargo ship that was torpedoed just out of port had 60,000 cases of beer aboard. It doesn't look like the liberty party will get any to drink.

December 5 — Received a Christmas package from home today, the candy was in fine condition.

December 8 — Pearl Harbor was attacked three years ago today. We sure have come a long way since then!

December 19 — Sea is very rough! We tried to refuel this morning but the sea was too rough. We made our approach up to the carrier USS Essex. We damaged our 40 mm, tore off our port side life rafts, ripped a good deal of the lifeline portside. It's a wonder it didn't sink us. We have only enough fuel left for 15 hours. Hope it lets up soon!!! No damage to personnel — thank God!

December 20 - Three cans were lost in the storm — they broke radio silence today- two were dead in the water, one was making 5 knots. The USS Hall turned over, broken in half, sank due to the storm. Ten enlisted men were picked up yesterday. Last night we were cautioned to keep a sharp lookout for survivors. At about 10:20 PM five officers including the skipper and 36 enlisted men were picked up after a day and a night on life rafts.

December 21 — Christmas just being around the corner received wife's letter yesterday — all's well back home thank God!

December 25 — Last night Christmas Eve, was as close as I could come to Christmas out here. I received two packages from Emma. I'm going to church services on the Dixie in the morning.

January 1 — Well a New Year is here, 1945.

January 10 — Sea became very rough at 3:00 AM!! We had good weather to attack Formosa. Landing on Luzon took place on the ninth. We were to engage any aircraft or naval forces that should happen to come out for battle. We are heading to attack Indochina through Hong Kong!! We are refueling the morning.

January 11 — We are headed at full speed to Omerack Bay. Adm. Nimitz's reported from Pearl Harbor, "Tomorrow you will make naval history. I know you boys will do a good job. Throw everything you have at them. God bless you." Several carriers and battle wagons (Jap) are reported to be in the harbor. We sent out some propaganda today from MacArthur's headquarters. Luzon radio — he stated that our carrier-based aircraft are out of reach to contact fleet so they won't suspect we were to attack at dawn. If made successful it will be a Pearl Harbor to the Japs. We attack Formosa day after tomorrow. We will hit them hard!!

January 12 — we went to GQ at dawn. Our planes took off for the first strike. We had a field day on the ships in port. We sank 28 ships. We are steaming north to north China Sea. We refuel tomorrow then attack Hong Kong!!

January 14 — The ship jumped so far out of the water last night it threw several of us out of our racks. It felt like she was going to break in half. I ran in shorts for the ladders!! It was really a scare now that we know it's not impossibility for cans to capsize and break in half. We sank seven convoy ships — troop transports — trying to reinforce Luzon — good!

January 20 — On the 15th we picked up dead Jap in water — we took him forward to see if he had any papers on him, he didn't! We are headed back to the Pacific.

January 21 — They are sure on our tail!!!! We went to GQ at 3:30 AM. The bogey turned out to be an Army B- 24. We almost open fired on him. We were taking on fuel fore and aft when there was a heavy explosion off our port quarter. The Langley had been hit by a bomb! Two Jap planes snuck over the Task Force, just then GQ sounded. I ran to mount the two torpedo tubes at my battle station expecting him to crash dive on us as he was headed our way. The wagons opened up, he dipped and one of our planes was on his tail! The F6F got him 8000 yards away! Just then the other dove on the carrier USS Ticonderoga. Our AA fire discouraged anymore attempts to get to us. Smoke and flames came up from the hangar deck! Once again I got the sick feeling when the perimeter went down! We downed 17 Jap planes in the next hour! Maddox, a can, on picket duty had a Jap suicide pilot come down on its deck! It did not go down as first reported to us. Men trapped by fire had just jumped over the side of the Ticonderoga. We picked up two men, one being an officer. The officer went over the side without a life jacket! We stopped to pick up the seamen while Jap planes were overhead. They said the Jap had dropped the bomb before she hit! In about 2 hours the fire on the carrier was under control! But many were reported dead and injured. A second suicide pilot dove into the bridge and hit the radar. The flight deck was smashed and the hangar deck a wreck! But she still kept her speed!

February 12 — We just learned as announced from the bridge we are to make a two day raid on Tokyo! The first carrier-based air raid on Tokyo since the start of the war!

We will go in quite close. I think this will be our bad operation. I hope to pull through all right — we will with the help of the Lord!

February 13 — Well three more days and we will hit Tokyo. I sure hope we take them by surprise.

February 16 — ... Our planes took off for Tokyo! We put 500 planes in the air! We launched strikes all day! Total damage is not yet known but you can be well assured it's plenty!

February 17 — I have the 4-8 watch! We're now waiting for GQ to sound. Our planes begin takeoff at dawn. I sure don't want to get sunk out here of all the places a man wouldn't stand a chance in this water!

February 18 — Several rounds were fired at enemy surface craft by the other cans in our picket. We fired several rounds 525 to be exact at Japs. They returned our fire. We then came in close and fired 40 mm. They returned fire with 3 inch. We took a 3 inch hole in the 40 mm and 20 mm magazine. It started on fire. Shells started exploding. I couldn't leave my battle station which was right over it. Smoke and flames came pouring out shells started exploding. We opened up on her (the Jap). She reloaded 50 and 30 mm guns. They sure were close. She steamed across our bow fired and hit us forward in the Chief's quarters and gun #1–5". Red Allman was killed — he never knew what hit him! The lighting system was shot up forward so they were in darkness, several fellows stumbled over something and finally someone stopped to look just as lights went on and it was Cook. He was dead. Several others were injured with shrapnel metal. The forward magazine was flooded a large hole ripped in #1- 5". Several holes in Chief quarters. We had to throw all the ammo over board. We held funeral services this morning at daylight. After it was all over I got down on my knees and thanked the Lord for seeing me through. Most of the crew was silent. Tomorrow will be another hectic day I suppose!

February 19 — Today was D-day for the island of Iwo Jima. We sighted it at dawn! We blew up an ammo dump earlier this morning. It shot flames up hundreds of feet in the air. The wagons lobbied shell after shell into the beach. The landing was made at 10 AM while we continued to fire up further on the mountain. Tanks got ashore. The Japs however returned fire. Planes dove on attack at the airfield and they didn't get a single plane in the air. The horizon is covered with supply ships waiting to go in as soon as a positive beach is established. Last night we expended 2200 rounds of 40 mm and more than 500 rounds of 5 inch. We took four 3 inch holes forward setting the Chiefs quarters on fire and one 3 inch back aft. Several holes are in us by machine gun fire. We will shell the beach all night. I figure the Japs will try to counter attack tonight as they usually try to.

February 22 — The Bridge just announced that we are to rejoin the task 58. We attack Tokyo area the 25th and 26th. We return south back here to Iwo Jima take ship back to Pearl Harbor! That means home — I hope! Reports last night were that the Marines are in the worst battle they have had in 165 years!! The Saratoga (carrier) took a fish. They are picking up survivors now.

February 25 — We picked up a pilot (fighter) this afternoon. He circled the carrier twice. He couldn't put his wheels down and his wing flaps wouldn't go down. He had to land in the water at full speed. He was stunned a little but no other damage except his plane which was shot up badly.

Fritz's journal continues to describe the daily encounters of his ship and the Task Force involved in the heavy fighting in the Pacific. Each entry carefully details the intense fighting in excruciating detail. On the 27th of March Fritz indicates that he observed 300 B-29s overhead at dawn returning from a bombing raid on Japan. At 3 PM the call came in and the ship picked up 24 radioman off the communication ship to take them to Guam. It was his hope that they would head home from there. In his March 30th entry, he notes that the ship is indeed headed for Guam convoy. On April 12th he records that ship took on provisions and that they were expecting to leave for Pearl Harbor. His last three entries reflect his excitement.

April 14 — we arrived at Pearl Harbor at 11:30 AM. We leave for Frisco tomorrow at 9 AM. Received a great deal of mail them home — first we've had since February!

April 15 — We're heading out of the harbor! We have a homeward bound pennant flying from the mainmast and it reaches from the mast to the fantail. A star for each officer and a foot of red and white for each member of the crew. We expect to get in Frisco on the 21st.

April 20 — will be in the USA in the morning. All hands will turn to unloading ammo and we have torpedoes and depth charges to get off. My leave starts May 12th!!

With the dropping of the atomic bombs and the surrender of Japan, World War II was over. I would like to say everyone lived happily ever after but that would not be true. Fritz was greatly impacted by the war and his Navy experiences for the rest of his life. Perhaps he suffered from Post Traumatic Stress Disorder. As with so many others, not only were the veterans left with the nightmares of engagement with the enemy and not knowing from one moment to the next whether they would ever come home, but family and loved ones that lived with the veterans after the war were also impacted in so many ways. War affects not only the men and women who served; it impacts on family and loved ones. I salute Fritz and all the members of the 'greatest generation' that served and fought in World War II.

As the years pass, the memories dim, the mist of time blurs the vision, I better understand the many different sides of Uncle Fritz and the way he lived his life after the war a little bit better now as I read his daily journal of the war. I still have not figured out many things. Why he did not move his family into the new house he built on Orcus Island? Why was he so strict with his three boys? Why did he continue to live in that little house which was as small as the home he grew up in when the new house he built was just a few hundred feet away in a beautiful park like setting? So many more questions with no apparent answers ...

But the one thing I do know for certain is why he thought we were careless and sloppy when we painted the trim on his cabin — because by Fritz's standards and expectations, we were!

The Lost Uncle — Brother Paul

Uncle Paul was more like a brother than an uncle to me. He was eight years older and we grew up living together in the house on Emerson Street. It was his parents' and my grandparents' home. After my grandparents adopted me when I was seven, Paul always referred to me as his "kid brother." We lived in a predominately Italian neighborhood and the big kids my age knew not to pick on me because they were aware that Paul was my big brother and they would have to answer to him for any misdeeds. There were a few times he went out of his way to protect me. I had a "free pass" to assert myself that none of the other kids enjoyed and, if a physical challenge arose out confrontations, all I had to say was, "I'll tell Paul if you..."

When I was in elementary school my mother, who I thought was my sister, was living with us and both she and my grandparents worked during the day so that left Paul and me on our own in the mornings. He had the responsibility for making sure that I got to school on time and he would ride the bus with me to School #43, then drop me off and be on his way to Jefferson High. Every morning Paul would wake me up and make sure I was dressed and ready for school and then he would make breakfast for us. Breakfast always revolved around bread. Usually it was piles of toast made in the gas oven with the swing out broiler grill which allowed for a large quantity to be made quickly at once. Then we would smother the toast in either one of a variety of Gram's home-made jams or jellies or we would tear it up into little pieces, put them in a bowl and add sugar and milk for homemade cereal as we called it. The same question was asked each morning, "Do you want cereal or toast or both?"

Every school morning thirty-five cents was left on the table so that I could buy a school lunch. That did not matter as Paul would make two sandwiches for each of us and pack them in brown lunch bags to be taken to school. On the opposite corner of school on Lyell Avenue stood a small neighborhood grocery store where we would arrive early and congregate with other kids before school opened. My lunch money was used to purchase two bottles of soda, my favorite, Pee-Wee Grape and Paul's, Pepsi, because it was twice as big as a bottle of Coke. We also bought two Hershey chocolate candy bars and there was even money left over for me to buy an ice cream in the cafeteria at lunch time if I so chose. Paul and I would enjoy our sodas and candy bars before the 5 minute school warning bell rang and then he was off to catch the city bus to his school leaving me alone to scoot across the cross walk with the school guard who was waving the throng of store groupies on to the school side walk. Our morning treats at the corner store was interrupted one day when Gram came wheeling her big brown '37 Chevy sedan around the corner and I was standing alone outside in front of the store enjoying my Pee-Wee grape soda while Paul was already on his way to catch his bus. I never noticed the car or Gram and I certainly was not on the lookout for her as I had assumed everyone was at work.

That evening at dinner Gram asked me if I enjoyed my soda that morning before school. How did she know? I looked over at Paul and he was silent and staring at nothing. He was not going to bail me out or help me in any way on this one as he usually did due to the guilty circumstances. I was busted! I knew a "Yes" or "No" to Gram's question was a confession on my part. I wanted Paul to answer but he was still starring out into space and I knew we were both in trouble. Dinner that evening marked the end of our morning visits to the store and Paul's bagged lunches for me for the rest of that school year. I really missed his lunches because he made huge peanut butter and homemade jam or jelly sandwiches that I used to trade for more interesting lunches. I could have homemade jelly or jam sandwiches any time at home but my friends in the lunch room were not so lucky. At lunch when the bags were taken out of the cubbies, most of them had large translucent oil stains on both sides of the bag from the homemade meat ball, fried egg, or egg plant sandwiches, or homemade cookies they contained. They never had the kind of big thick sandwiches that Paul made for me and I never had anything like what they had in their bags. I usually could negotiate a whole fried egg or meatball sandwich with red sauce for a half of one of mine. Better yet, I would trade one of my sandwiches for a dime which could be used to buy an ice cream! Paul's lunches were THAT good!

One school morning both of us got up earlier than normal, finished breakfast and had some time to kill before we had to leave for school. We decided that even if the rule was that we couldn't play ball in the house we could toss a few around and I could try out the old catcher's mitt and who would ever know? It was a great game we had going until I threw the ball too high and too hard and it hit the ceiling in just the perfect spot. Well not just THE perfect spot but the place where an old ceiling light fixture used to be located before it was removed and the hole covered over when the ceiling was painted. The ball hit just right and the hole reappeared. Panic set in and Paul sent me looking for masking tape, an old Christmas gift box and to the basement for the can of ceiling paint and a paint brush. Before we had collected all necessary repair materials I had to leave for school alone and Paul stayed to finish the job. That afternoon I rushed home from school to inspect the ceiling and it looked good to me. After dinner my Dad followed his usual routine and retired to the living room to read the evening paper and then listen to the radio. When I finished and went into the living room he asked me what happened to the ceiling. Paul was not home in time for supper and I was on my own so I explained the situation taking the least possible responsibility and tried damage control. It didn't matter, I was busted AGAIN!

I was ten years old and five years had already passed since the end of WWII but all the kids in the neighbor hood were still interested in playing 'war'. Our favorite war game was "bombs over Tokyo." Our war games impacted Paul in at least two ways. Being older, he had his own group of friends and they had built a playhouse or what boys call a fort or hut. It was a collection of old scrap wood and tarpaper nailed together with an old wooden door and two open windows. One day my group of friends and I were using the fort pretending we were fighting the "Japs" and we had to call in the air force to drop bombs on the enemy. In the imagination of ten year olds the enemy had taken over the fort and we had to bomb them to drive them out into the open to shoot them. After what seemed like a couple of hours of searching for and collecting the biggest rocks we could carry, we managed to get them all up on the roof. Bombing commenced with the rocks held over head and then throwing them down to the roof and before long the tar paper and wood gave way and ripped and a board cracked or broke here and there and finally the 'bombs' were making their way through the roof and we were successful in driving the enemy out into the open. Brother Paul was not impressed with the hole in the roof of his fort and was heartbroken it was ruined. He could not understand why we would ruin his beautiful fort, the one that was our refuge when it was raining. At the time the successful bombing mission made perfect sense to me.

During the 1940's and early '50's, in our neighborhood and in our families, large toys were expensive, rare, and if you were lucky enough to have one, there was usually only one. Paul had a large WWII Jeep metal toy that he had when he was much younger and saved it. It was in outstanding perfect condition. On a rainy day I was going through a storage dresser in the cellar way and found the Jeep. I didn't know whose it was. After school I was always left on my own before my grandparents and my mom got home from work which was always well after 5 o'clock. I showed my friends the toy Jeep I found and we all thought it would make our war games even more exciting, especially if it suffered a direct hit from a bomb. Yes, indeed, the huge rocks held overhead were very effective 'bombs' and destroyed the enemy's Jeep. I left it out by the back steps after we were through playing with it only to have it be discovered by Paul when he returned home after school and work. He was heartbroken once again about what we did to his Jeep and told Gram. She was also upset with me and we had a long talk. I apologized to Paul and he was gracious about the incident but I don't think he ever really did get over the hurt. Years later, always with a smile, he would remind me in a kidding fashion about my destruction of his Jeep. Paul was in his 70's when I found a steel toy Jeep almost identical to the one he had as a child. I gave it to him as a sort of gag gift and also a serious apology gift one Christmas. He was stunned and I think I saw a tear in his eyes. He was pleased but I know in my heart of hearts it didn't replace the one he lost. He had it on display on his fireplace mantel for a year or two and then it disappeared from sight and I never saw it again. Brother Paul, I am sincerely sorry: my only wish is that I could have written this for you to read before it was your time to leave us.

Paul never finished high school, married at 18, and worked at Delco Products and a monument company as an engraver all his life. He was very proud of me as I became firmly established in my career in public education. He always would tell his friends when I was with him, "This is my kid brother!" And then he would go on and tell them something about where I worked or what my position was and that I had a Ph.D.. He was so proud of me and loved me and I loved him as a brother loves a brother!

The Farmer in the Dell

The refrain to the old 19th century hymn *"Revive Us Again"* is:

Hallelujah! Thine the glory.
Hallelujah! Amen.
Hallelujah! Thine the glory.
Revive us again.

New words were sung by a veteran solider returning from WWII. I know this because my grandmother was standing next to him and his new bride as he sang at the top of his voice that Sunday in the tiny church on Lee Road the following:

Hallelujah! Thine the glory.
Hallelujah! I'm a bum.
Hallelujah! Thine the glory.
Revive me again.

Erma and George moved to their farm as newlyweds in 1947. George served in the army for the full duration of WWII, enlisting in January of 1941 before the attack on Pearl Harbor when the US entered the war. Erma was my mother's younger sister by three years. During the war, she worked in Bellingham, Washington at the Boeing aircraft manufacturing plant just like many other "Rosie the Riveters." George and Erma first met in Rochester before he enlisted in the Army. They wrote love letters to each other through 4 long years. I was perhaps 10 when I found those letters in a shoe box in the upstairs attic of their old farm house. That is when Erma took them to the burn barrel out behind the house, thus liberating them through the purification of fire. In 1945, while living in Washington State, Erma received information that George was going to be transferred state side to Fort Lewis in Seattle for a brief time before being sent on to Fort Dix in New Jersey for discharge. While living and working at the air craft factory, she lived in a rented room with a family in Bellingham. Erma asked the husband and wife if they would drive her to Seattle to see if by any chance they could locate George. The Fort was huge, busy and very crowded, but while the three of them were waiting in a civilian holding area, an announcement came over the PA system ordering Private George Spears to report to a special area. Through that public announcement, they found each other for a brief but magical reunion. After George's orders finally arrived, he and all the other soldiers traveled by train to Fort Dix, New Jersey.

As soon as he was discharged, he boarded another train and once again he found himself traveling across the country; this time in the opposite direction and bound for northwest US with Bellingham as his destination. Just 45 days after his discharge from the military, George and Erma were married on the 19th of October, 1945. During his time in the military, George sent his entire Army paychecks home to his mother Florence with instructions that she should find and purchase a farm for him. It was in 1942 when she bought a 100 acre abandoned farm for $1,200. After the wedding, this was to be the farm that they moved to after a brief stay with his grandparents who lived in the area. With the winter season and no heat or water available in the old farm house, they spent that winter living with George's grandparents and helping with the work on their farm. That spring Erma and George worked to get the house ready to live in and moved to their own farm up in the hills of Cameron, NY.

I believe that George was impacted by the war in countless ways and it is my conjecture that he suffered from post-traumatic stress syndrome. This is a fairly new term and diagnosis that we are familiar with today. At the end of WWII it was unknown or, at the very least, unrecognized or not admitted. The Army trained him as a heavy machine gunner and he served in the Western Pacific in many of the major battles including the assault on the Gilbert and Marshal Islands, Tinian, Saipan, and finally, Okinawa. In these island invasions, he was exposed to ghastly and horrendous fighting; an unimaginable loss of life through the relentless resistance of the Japanese to protect the islands coupled with the fact that surrender by the Japanese was not usually a cultural viable option. It was fight to the death, never surrender. All George experienced was the death that surrounded him during the furious fighting. He was 31 years old when he was honorably discharged, considerably older than the majority of the other veterans. I sense that his age and his war experiences had a major impact on the development of his personality, attitudes, outlook, and life goals when the war ended.

George had great plans for developing the abandoned farm that Erma and he moved to after their marriage as evidenced by creating a very large spring fed farm pond and adopting the latest land management concepts such as contour farming. He also tested soil samples and added essential fertilizers to improve the fields for planting. He modernized the dairy barn, added a pneumatic milking machine, and built a new milk house for a cold water storage tank for milk cans. He also constructed a cement silo to improve winter feed and storage for the dairy herd. The large new barn addition was well planned but unfinished due to lack of finances and time which I presume had to be a major disappointment for him. I imagine George was hopeful that his oldest child of seven young ones, and the only male, would one day work side by side with him as a partner on the farm and complete all the dreams, plans, building and development that he wanted but was unable to finish.

When his son Dale was killed in an automobile accident it became evident to George his dreams for the farm were not going to become reality. His sadness, disappointment, and bitterness exhibited itself in his interactions with his spouse Erma and their six younger daughters. The family members were not treated well in the latter years by George. When the old farm house was no longer a viable abode for the family, he under took the challenge as well as the necessity of building a new home for them without having enough money to do so. It took a long time to come to fruition. This was accomplished in part by tearing down the old farm house and using the lumber to build the new one. Money was so scarce and lacking that the old nails had to be pulled out of the boards, straighten by hand and reused. An alternate place for the family to live had to be found for several years while the new house was being built. The family moved into an old one room school house across the road which was a part of the farm. Winters there were cold and the only heat came from a pot belly wood burning stove. The old school house had no insulation and the winters in the hills were cold, severe, and lengthy.

Life was difficult for everyone; however, George and Erma persevered and were able to move in to a newly built home even although it was not totally finished. George then took on the challenge of building a new barn under the same conditions, that is, lack of finances and time. The larger addition planned but not completed to the old barn was abandoned. A new barn was planned and construction started on a one story building that was scaled down in size compared to the old one. The dairy herd was sold and the new plan for farming was to raise heifers from young calves for sale before they freshened. It was apparent to me that all of this took a toll in terms of frustration and stress which I am sure the family members felt in so many different ways. It also took a physical toll on George and his heart and he entered the VA hospital from which he did not return shortly before the new barn was finished.

Life on the farm was very demanding for the young married couple and from the beginning, they struggled financially. Nonetheless, by 1948, George and Erma made additional land purchases which resulted in the farm's total acreage being expanded to 383 acres. Over the years they had seven children, the first born in 1946 with one new baby every two years through 1954 and then an additional two children after that. Their firstborn was a son named Dale and he was only a year old when I, a 7 year old city boy, began visiting the farm. My aunt treated me as a member of her family and the children were like siblings to me. As the oldest, I spent a great deal of my time as their babysitter during the day.

The farm was of great significance to George. I think that having survived the war, he felt liberated to live his life from that point onward, just as he chose. They began their married life together with the equity of an abandoned farm and a well-worn barn and farmhouse, all needing attention and modernization. The first priority of any dairy farmer is to build up his herd of cows for the production of milk since this equates to income, but it is also necessary to plant and harvest crops to provide for the livestock during the winter months. There was never enough time in a day to do all the farm work required as well as to undertake the repairs needed for the barn, house, and farm machinery.

In 1947, they bought a new Allis Chalmers tractor and so began their ongoing struggle to make improvements and create a successful farming operation. From the very beginning, there was always more work than one person could possibly manage and Erma gladly assisted with tractor work as her time allowed. She was not interested in working the dairy barn, milking cows or any of the other endless daily routines requiring feeding and watering the animals. I have a clear picture in my mind of her on the seat of the tractor with her huge pregnant belly just barely clearing the steering wheel, driving in the hay fields with a piece of farm equipment behind. However, the expanding family did not allow a great deal of time free from household chores or child rearing for assisting with the needed field work.

Eventually, lack of capital and finances for farm operations and improvements took their toll and Erma assisted with the badly needed cash flow by securing a job at the General Electric manufacturing plant in Bath. Eventually she became a night shift supervisor at the plant. Still, operating expenses for the farm were so great that George also had to secure a full-time position. He started working at the Ingersoll-Rand plant. With a full time position, there was precious little time left for farm work. In order for both the family and the farm to survive there were no other viable options. George would milk the cows early in the morning before going to his factory job and again late at night after returning home. As soon as his son was old enough and able, he helped in the barn milking cows and with the field work. Erma worked the night shift so there was a period of time during the summer days when I took responsibility for supervising and 'playing' with the younger children to keep them occupied and busy. I spent all my school vacations on the farm.

The smells are as dramatic today in my memory as they were seven decades ago: fresh ozone in the air after a severe summer thunderstorm, the sweet smell of new mown hay, damp rich earth from plowed ground, warm cow's milk fresh from the udder, new hay in the barn loft, wet wool on sheep after a rain storm, and a newly whitewashed dairy barn. As a youngster, my family lived in the city but, from the time I was 7 years old until I left home for college, my school vacations and summers were spent on Aunt Erma's and Uncle George's farm.

I was about 12 when I expressed my desire to spend time on the tractor to assist with the farm work. George was very careful to give me safety instructions and he provided a trial period under his supervision to see how things would work out. All went well during the testing period, and after this I spent hours on the seat of the tractor, mowing hay and then raking it to get it ready for bailing. I also tilled the newly plowed fields with a set of drags to prepare the ground for planting. For me, it was not work at all, as I loved every minute on the little orange Allis-Chambers tractor.

Those farm summers were the best and worst of times. I immensely enjoyed any work that involved the tractor but it was difficult taking care of my younger cousins, particularly when they were in diapers. The time between when Erma left for her work and George returned home from his seemed to last an eternity when I was alone with the younger children. I do remember that I enjoyed making meals for my cousins and myself, being creative with what I could find in the cupboard and fridge. I made the famous "Buehler Triple Decker Sandwiches" as the kids called them. I also made taffy once in awhile which they also enjoyed. I knew that money and finances were tricky, with never enough for new shoes or clothes or even groceries at times, and this often left me feeling a bit gloomy. I also recall many happy times and it was a very joyful day when my two oldest cousins sold the largest number of subscriptions for the local town newspaper and won two new bicycles. As the younger children grew up, those bikes were passed down as soon as the next child was big enough to learn to ride. From my summers on the farm, I learned many lessons for life about what a struggle it is when you do not have enough money and how sharing what you have with others can make such a difference.

I also learned about work ethic and how to do a job the right way the first time. George was very proud of his farm and wanted everything done the right way but he struggled with this all the time because he was pulled in so many directions by the amount of work and the lack of time and finances to make it all happen. Uncle George taught me the proper way to mow hay. After I had spent a day in one of the hay fields, he returned home from work to inspect the job I had just completed. He was not pleased seeing that some of the hay stalks were still standing and had not been cleanly cut down. He explained that when I hit rock with the sickle bar, it nicked one of the teeth and this resulted in not cutting the hay stalk cleanly, particularly at the corners of each swatch. That evening, he taught me how to remove the sickle bar from the tractor, sharpen the teeth on a grinder, and how to remove a broken tooth and replace it if it could not be sharpened. Thereafter, every day when I took a break for lunch, I disassembled the sickle bar and sharpened each and every tooth. Changing a broken tooth on the bar was very difficult so I was cautious not to hit any stones in the field. How to do your work well is not a bad thing for a young teenager to learn.

I enjoyed the farm and more importantly the tractor so much that I thought I wanted to be a farmer. George rarely left the farm because as a dairy farmer you have a responsibility to milk your herd every morning and evening, but one summer, when I was just turning 15, it was time for them to buy another older used car. Erma encouraged George to take a weekend off so they could go to Rochester to purchase a car that her brother Fritz had told them about and also visit with their family members who lived in the area while they were there. They both asked me if I thought I could handle taking care of the animals while they were gone and of course I said yes. All the children went with them so I had no additional responsibilities other than to water and feed the animals in the barn and to milk the cows. I was sure there would be no problems.

Cows are remarkable critters. Somehow, they knew that they were being treated in a different manner by a person with smaller and smoother hands than what they were used to. I used the milking machine on each cow and I thought I was successful in judging if they were completely milked out but apparently I was mistaken. When the milking machine is taken off a cow's udder, the procedure is to milk them just a bit by hand for a minute or two to ensure that there is no milk left. Did I mention that cows are fascinating animals? It seems that bovines are not completely contented with someone who might be a little nervous about the hand milking part. They are actually able to hold back some of their milk if they desire or are nervous. This does not make for a good scenario. The other element to consider when milking a cow happens to be that their tails are always flying back and forth to keep the flies off their backs or, in my opinion, to swat the person doing the milking across the face. This wet tail is as offensive as it is aggravating considering where it's been and what it's been in! Maybe I was not quite as careful as I should have been with the hand milking part of the operation. I believe it was right then and there that I decided I did not want to become a farmer. Unfortunately, when bovines are not completely milked they run the risk of developing mastitis, an inflammation caused by bacteria in the retained milk. The end result is not pretty.

When a farmer's milk is being sold to the milk plant for processing, it is tested for bacteria and if it tests positive, all the milk from that farm has to be dumped. Dumped milk equals no money. Three of George's best producing milk cows had mastitis, thus a bacterial infection after I cared for them that fateful weekend. Both George and Erma were kind and appreciated my effort to assist with the milking but that did not ease my conflicted feelings of guilt and incompetence. Considering the inexpensive used car they brought home, it turned out to be a very expensive trip to Rochester.

In many ways, those farm experiences shaped me and who I became. Some of those experiences I try desperately to forget and others are a pleasure or even a thrill to recall. But the one thing I now understand better after all these years are George's supplemental words he added to the refrain of the old gospel hymn:

Hallelujah! Thine glory.
Hallelujah! I'm a bum.
Hallelujah! Thine the glory.
Revive me again.

How Did He Know?

It was December 1952 and I was 12 years old. It was also the last week of school before Christmas break. Our class had just finished a history unit highlighting the tenth anniversary of WWII. As a class, we listened to recordings of the speeches of President Roosevelt and Prime Minister Winston Churchill played on a record machine's turn table from the school's AV Department. By the show of hands, we responded to the questions Miss Price asked of us inquiring about our brothers or any other family members that may have served in the military during the war. The fighting seemed to have happened so long ago that we could not figure out why Miss Price was making such a big deal about all of this. Didn't she know Christmas was coming and we just wanted to talk about our upcoming and long overdue vacation from school? The only thing we were all thinking about and wishing for was what our best present would be on Christmas morning. Most of the boys even wondered if Miss Price knew about Christmas and if anyone in her family would have a present for her. We didn't even know if she had any family at all; we thought that she was so old that everyone in her family had probably already died. I remember feeling sad and I thought I could ask my grandmother to bake some extra Christmas cookies for her and that I could bring to school. I was sure Miss Price would like to know that she did not miss out on the joy of Christmas. By the time I got home from school on that last day I had forgotten all about the cookies.

It seemed as if Friday afternoon would never arrive when my mother got out of work and she, grandma, and I would drive almost 3 hours to the farm. I already had plans that I would spend every day of Christmas vacation with Aunt Erma and Uncle George. I knew my mother would have to drive back to the city Sunday night so she could go to work on Monday morning and then return on Christmas Eve day and spend Christmas and perhaps another day or two with us before having to drive back to the city for work once again.

As soon as my mom got home from General Motors Corporation we loaded the trunk of her car with suitcases, bags of food, cookies, and bags of presents for my cousins. We had a quick bite to eat and we were off. It was late in the evening when we drove through the deep snow drift at the end of driveway at the farm. We were greeted by Aunt Erma's three children who were still up and in their pajamas anxiously awaiting our arrival. Excitement was in the air as we unloaded the car and carried everything into the kitchen of the old farm house. We moved close to the wood stove and warmed our hands and stomped the snow off our shoes and boots. The floor was too cold to walk on in stocking feet so we stayed by the door on the rug near the stove waiting for the snow to melt off our boots and for them to dry a bit. There was excitement in the air. We had some hot cocoa and Aunt Erma brought out a plate of freshly baked Christmas cookies she had just frosted. Uncle George thought it would be a great idea and a treat for everyone if Auntie made some fudge. As our feet were drying she mixed up the ingredients by hand in a bowl and then poured the mixture in a pan and set it on the stove. She always made the best fudge in our family. The smell of chocolate filled the air as the dark sugary mixture began to bubble in the sauce pan. Then she buttered a glass baking dish to be used to pour the cooked mixture into to cool and then cut into squares. Someone had to clean the spoon and cooking pan after the fudge was poured and scraped into the glass dish. This was my task and a most delightful one to be shared with my three younger cousins.

Frosted and decorated cookies followed by hot fudge and ice cold milk is a wonderful way to prepare children for bedtime and a restful night's sleep. The next morning arrived bright, clear, sunny, and very cold. The upstairs bedroom where I slept had no heat but under a mountain of blankets and quilts I was as warm as toast. I could see my breath when I was called for breakfast so the order of the day was to jump out of bed, grab my clothes and dress as quickly as possible without

103

standing on the cold floor in bare feet. It took just a moment to do this while running down the stairs still buttoning my shirt. Pancakes and eggs were on the table that morning and the smells in the kitchen were wonderful. I hurried over to the kitchen stove to try to get warm before sitting down for this entire wonderful banquet.

After breakfast my Aunt suggested that perhaps finding, selecting, and cutting down a Christmas tree would be a great morning adventure. That venture would commence only after I completed my assigned chore which was to fill the wood box in the back room. It was important that the kitchen stove had enough wood for the day and into the evening until it was to be filled once again the following morning. I dressed warmly and then carried in the wood from the pile which was located about half way to the barn. After five trips with my arms full of wood, the individual pieces seemed to get heavier and the pile of wood by the bucksaw seemed to be much further in distance from the house than when I started. It seemed to take forever before the box was full and stacked higher than its sides, but eventually my Aunt was pleased with the supply of wood in the back room.

She asked me to go to the barn to ask Uncle George where I could find a saw to use to cut down the perfect tree. She also instructed me to make sure the tree should be evenly shaped and as full as possible. I was told to avoid the thin skimpy trees. I found my Uncle in the barn and received instructions on how to cut down the tree and to avoid hitting the ground with the saw thereby dulling the blade. I was also told where to go to get the best tree which was up on the side hill in the woods near the property line fence but not to go on the other side of the fence. Back to the house I went to warm up again and my Aunt then informed me that Dale, my younger cousin wanted to go with me to cut down the Christmas tree. It took Dale awhile to find his outdoor clothes and to begin dressing and, in the meantime, I was fully dressed and not only getting warm, I was beginning to sweat. Grandma came to Dale's aid and bundled him up so he looked exactly like Pillsbury's Dough Boy with a scarf around his face with only his eyes showing below his knitted wool hat.

Off we went on a long hike down the hill behind the house to the pond. The pond was frozen and we spent some time on the ice, clearing it with our boots, making paths, sliding around on it, and then walked across the pond to the dike, climbed the dike, and walked to the bottom of the hill. We had a barbwire fence to climb over or under without getting our mittens, pants, hats, or jackets caught. Then it was up the steep hill to the top. It was a long hike through the deep snow and when we arrived at the top we sat down to rest. Having already been in wet clothes in the house while Dale was dressing and now with both of us soaked from playing in the snow and on the ice and adding the fact that we were perspiring while climbing the hill, we were both not only wet but now very cold.

As we moved on into the woods looking for the perfect tree we realized these trees, as we were to find out later, were Scotch pines and as such were pretty barren trees as far as possible from what one would expect a perfect Christmas tree look like. The woods were thick with growth and the trees were small. As we studied the situation I thought the taller trees were much fuller at their tops. That's when we figured out the best thing we could do to get the perfect Christmas tree was to just cut down one of the tall ones and then chop the top off and we would then have the picture perfect tree to take home. That was the plan so I began to saw back and forth on a tree that was about 8 inches in diameter at the base. It was not an easy task. Dale and I took turns using the saw.

At first it was fairly easy until we cut half way through the trunk and the weight of the tree began to bird the saw blade. I finally worked the blade free and out of the cut we had made and I started sawing from the other side of the trunk. After a period of time working the saw back and forth, the tree was starting to lean and with a few more passes of the saw, Dale hollered, "Timber!" and slowly the tree started to fall. It didn't quite make it to the ground as it landed on top of another pine tree. I had to climb up on the fallen tree to saw the top off which I had apparently misjudged where to saw it by quite a bit. When we finally had the tree top free and on the ground and stood it up in the snow it was about four and a half feet tall which was shorter than I was. To add insult to injury the tree top wasn't that much fuller that most of the other smaller trees all around us. I heard my Aunt's faint voice off in the distance calling our names. We shouted as loud as we could and told her we were OK and that we had the tree and were coming home.

Both Dale and I were exhausted as we dragged our perfect tree down the hill to the first fence we had to climb over or crawl under. It was all we could do to get the tree over the top strand of barbwire. Then we both had to get over the fence ourselves without getting our clothes or mittens caught on any of the barbed wires. Dragging the tree across the ice on the pond was not as easy as dragging it down the steep hill because we had gravity assisting us on the down side of the hill. Dragging it up the other smaller hill from the pond to the farm house was another matter altogether. It was difficult but somehow we managed, even though we were exhausted and almost couldn't make it through the deep snow. We managed to get it to the back porch, up the steps, and then I called my Aunt to come out and see our perfect tree. She smiled with approval and told us what a wonderful job we had done. Then she invited us into the warm kitchen and had us take off all our wet clothes. She wrapped each of us in a blanket and sat us down at the table and served us a huge bowl of hot tomato soup and toasted cheese sandwiches. It was the best lunch I ever had!

Uncle George came in from the barn, looked at the tree on the back porch and told us he would make a stand for it after he had his lunch. He also told us he would get a wooden apple crate to set it on so it would be up high and off the floor in the living room. He explained that the apple crate would allow Santa room to pile the presents under the tree. He also asked us where we put the saw when we brought it back. Oh, the saw! We told him we forgot it and left it on the fence post on hill by where we cut the tree down. He said he would walk up and get it and I told him he didn't need to do that and that I would go and get it for him. I didn't want him to see the big tree we had cut down just for its top. As tired as I was I got dressed again and my clothes were still wet but I did have another pair of dry mittens. It was a long and cold walk down to the pond, over the wire fence, and up the side hill to retrieve the saw and even a longer and colder trip back to the house the second time.

When I returned I thought I was so clever until Uncle George asked me why I didn't just cut down a tree on the ground instead of sawing down a big tree and cutting the top off from it. He laughed and Aunt Erma smiled. How in the world did he know what took place way up on the side hill in the woods? We had a wonderful Christmas and Santa did bring everyone a present and placed them under the perfect tree.

Earl and the Willys

My earliest memory of Earl Townsend was seeing him driving along the road at a snail's pace delivering the mail at Uncle George's and Aunt Erma's farm. Earl drove just a little faster than I could push my wagon along the side of the road. As a matter of fact, on the long hill past the farm house going down the Gulf hill I could almost catch him by coasting in the wagon. Earl would deliver the mail late in the afternoon at each farm on the way home from the Cameron Post Office to where he lived in the little house at the end of the dirt road at the midway point on the hill.

During my Christmas vacation I was surprised to see Earl operating a large dozer and moving massive piles of snow, cutting through the snow drifts, and clearing the road so vehicles would be able to pass and make their way to town. When a large snow storm dumped several feet of snow and the town plow could not make it through the drifts or got stuck trying, the highway department would send out the town's only bulldozer to get the job done. There was Earl sitting on the open seat of that huge machine without a cab for protection bundled up against the bitter cold and blowing snow. I called out to Aunt Erma that I saw Earl Townsend out in front of the house clearing the road. She explained to me that one of Mr. Townsend's jobs was working for the highway department, building and repairing roads in the summer and plowing and clearing snow from the roads in the winter.

I was confused and I questioned my Aunt about this as I remembering seeing him delivering the mail in the summer and how could he be the mailman and at the same time work for the highway department? As Erma explained the details I began to realize a few of the differences between living in the city and in farm country. Earl did indeed work for the Town of Cameron Highway Department and he also had a contract with the US Post Office for a rural delivery route. The mail always made it to the country farms regardless of the storms and blizzards since he was responsible for the plowed the roads in the winter and could deliver the mail on the way home at the end of the day after plowing the country roads. The mail always was delivered, even in blizzard conditions. It was the one thing the farmers and their wives could depend on especially considering the US Post Office rural free delivery system, which allowed farm and household goods ordered from companies such as Sears Roebuck, Montgomery Ward's, and the GLF farm store. The mailman delivered the goods ordered which was as convenient for the farmers as it is for us today by driving to a shopping mall.

I was fascinated by the car that Earl drove and used to deliver the mail. It was a cute distinctive little gray 4-door 1939 Willys. I loved cars as a youngster and knew all of them by sight as well as by sound and I realized that Willys were a rare thing on the highway. When WWII began, the Willys Motor Company secured a contract with the government to manufacture vehicles for the war effort and these vehicles became known and loved by all as 'Jeeps'. After WWII ended in 1945 the Willys Motor Company continued to manufacture Jeeps and also the 4-wheel drive Jeepster which was a sporty version made for family use. Earl's 1939 Willys was an older car model no longer manufactured so I was intrigued by it and realized I really had never seen another one other than Earl's.

Earl drove that car until 1953 at which time I guess he decided to retire it and replace it with a newer more up to date vehicle, an older Ford truck. He parked the Willys in his side yard right next to the house. Whenever I drove the tractor to mow or rake hay on the upper hay fields of the farm I had to go directly by Earl's house on the way. One day going back to the farm house on the tractor after spending the day working in the fields, I noticed that Earl's truck was there and knew he was home from work so I stopped to talk to him to see what he was going to do with that old car of his. He told me that someday he would probably sell it. I asked him if he were to sell it, how much would he want for it? He replied, "Fifty dollars." I guess my reaction and the look on my face must have struck a chord in his heart as he cleared his throat and corrected himself and told me he meant to say twenty-five dollars. It didn't matter much either way as twenty-five dollars was exactly twenty-five dollars more than I had in my pocket or anywhere else for that matter. Totally ignoring my financial state of affairs, I told him I would buy the Willys from him and I shook his hand to validate the deal as I learned to do by watching farmers buy or sell a cow or calf. A point to ponder at this juncture is that in farm country in the 1950's a handshake was a contract which did not need to be reduced to writing. I had just made a legally binding deal with Earl to acquire his car and I had no money. I was in deep do-do and my personal integrity, honesty and morals were at stake with that hand shake.

What to do? I asked to go back home to Rochester where I collected old newspapers, iron, tin and steel to sell for scrap at the junk yard. With a few meager dollars earned from my collecting and with 'loans' from my aunt, grandmother, and mother, I had managed within two weeks to put together the twenty-five dollars I needed! The sleepless nights and the long days of worrying about the contract and my reputation were over as I walked down the road to Earl's house. He wasn't home and I thought long and hard on the walk back if I was ever going to own his car. There were two or three more long walks from the farm to Earl's place and back without catching him at home. Then one day when I was on the tractor on the way back from the hay field for lunch, I happened to spot Earl's 'new' truck parked in front of his home. I guessed that Earl was also home for lunch so I stopped. All I wanted was to own that Willys and drive it back to the farm as mine own car. If I had been thinking just a teeny tiny bit I would have figured out readily that Earl did not drive all the way home from Cameron just to have lunch. He never drove home for lunch! I walked up to the front door. Behind the screen door I could see that the wooden door was open but there was no sign of life. I knocked on the screen door. No answer. I knocked again. No answer. I could see his truck in the front yard so I knew he had to be home. I thought perhaps he didn't hear me the first couple of times so I pounded on the screen door. That is when I saw Earl coming to the door in just his underwear. His dark sun tanned face and his tanned arms below where he wore his the short sleeved shirts were in sharp contrast to the pasty white of the tops of his arms and the rest of all his thin tall body. Even at the age of 13 I instantly knew he wasn't home for lunch and not being dressed he wasn't home for a shower or bath. I also figured out that he didn't have his work clothes off because it was that dreadfully hot outside. Now what to do? Should I run? I froze and couldn't move or speak. Earl knew what I was there for and I slipped him the folded up dollar bills that I had in my hand through the screen door. I opened the screen door a couple of inches just to get my hand through and handed him the money as he was standing off to side so I couldn't see him and so there was no eye contact. He said ever so quickly that I could come back in the evening after 6:00 to get the registration and pick up the car as he didn't know where the registration and the keys were at the moment. That evening I waited until 7:00 just to be safe and walked the half mile to his place. It was a long walk and I time to think about what happened at lunch time and was embarrassed to even go up to the front screen door and knock. All I had in my mind at that moment was the vision of Earl in his underwear coming to the screen door earlier that afternoon and I wanted to get this deal done and get the hell out of there. When I finally did knock ever so lightly, Earl appeared at the door smiling as if nothing had ever happened and handed me the keys and registration, thanked me for the money and told me to be safe going back to the farm and to drive slowly. I drove the car at a snail's pace back up the hill to Aunt Erma's and Uncle George's farm and I had that wonderful feeling that life could never be any better than this, ever! What a feeling of joy, independence, and mini -adult. I still often wonder what Earl's thoughts of his day were with first my knocking and then my pounding on his door that summer afternoon.

Some two decades later Earl's and my path were to cross once again so to speak. I enjoyed the farm so much growing up that as an adult I wanted to buy some land on which to build a cabin. Uncle George told me about a 10 acre parcel of land adjacent to his upper farm acreage that might be for sale. He and I went to look at the boundaries and walk the land and I liked what I saw and decided to try to purchase it.

Earl had died some years prior to this and his widow wanted to move out of her and Earl's old house and relocate to the town of Bath. The owner of Ward's Feed Supply business had traded a small parcel of land with a mobile home on it that he owned for the property that Mrs. Townsend owned and she moved to town. When I spoke to Mr. Ward about the property and shared with him that my Uncle had told me it might be for sale he indicated he was willing to sell just the 10 acres across the road from the little house where the Townsends had lived. He wanted to keep an acre and the old Townsend house for himself since he had a renter living there. I was successful in purchasing the parcel and we built a year-round cabin on the land. The cabin was located just above the existing pond that Earl had built with the Town bulldozer all those years ago for use by the fire department. It is interesting how things work out over time. I thought of Earl in his underwear every time I drove by his old place on the way to our cabin in the woods and always with a slight curl on my lips and a little smile on my face.

Willys Race Day

Little did I appreciate the first car I was to own, a 1939 Willys 4-door sedan which, as it turns out, was a rare car when I acquired it. I wanted to make it into a stock car. Stock car racing was all the rage in the early 1950's. My Uncle Fritz and Paul had taken me to some stock car races at the Monroe County Fairgrounds and I was enthralled watching them. Most of the stock cars were old 1932-40 Fords along with a few odd Chevys that had been modified for racing. Modifications to these cars often included reducing the weight of the car by removing all unnecessary interior items including: upholstery, seats, window glass as well as exterior fenders and bumpers, or modifying them extensively. Additionally modifications consisted of building roll bars and heavy duty bumpers and of course, painting big numbers on the side of the car. In my mind, I had race car plans for this '39 Willys of what the car should look like from my observations of going to those few races at the fairgrounds.

Earl Townsend had owned his 1939 Willys since it was new. I doubt he ever drove it over 30 mph. He had a rural delivery route and used this car to deliver the mail every day. He was a town highway employee who operated the Town's heavy equipment and snowplow and was responsible for all truck and equipment maintenance and upkeep. He maintained his only source of transportation in the same careful way. I bought this wonderful old and rare car and tried to make a race car out of it following the methods already described. What a shame. All the dirt track race cars were called 'stock cars' and the races were referred to as 'stock car races.' These modified race cars usually were numbered with either one or two digits and these were painted boldly on the doors of the cars using digits 1 to 100. There were about a dozen cars in a race so there was no need to have a 3 digit number. While racing, the numbers on the cars allowed the spectators to quickly identify their favorite car, mechanic, and driver since the cars were listed in the printed bulletin by their number with all the detailed information about the car and race crew noted. I thought it would be clever to not use the traditional numbering method, so I painted large white numbers on each side of my 'race car' which was 144 ¼. No one ever used a three digit number let alone a fractional number and I liked the way the number 4 repeated itself.

Now it was time to test my race car minus the interior back seat, rear fenders and anything else I removed with a hammer, chisel, screw driver, a pair of pliers and an adjustable wrench. Since I had finished mowing and raking the field on the north side of the farm house and Uncle George had bailed the hay, I thought that if I gathered all the bales out of the field on the hay wagon and then unloaded them in the hay loft in the barn I would have a place to make a great oval race track to drive on. After two days of hard work, all the bales were in the barn. It never occurred to me that I should share my plans for the race track with anyone. Uncle George was pleased with my industrious effort and labor of getting the bales in to the barn while they were fresh and before they may have been rained on and ruined. Not sharing my plans for the field may have been mistake number Uno. I made a few passes around the 'track' when no one was around and it was great fun.

The next morning when Uncle George left the house to go to the upper farm to get the cows to the barn for milking, I made my move. There was a heavy dew on the stubble left in the hay field and I discovered, quite by accident, that by going as fast as I could in an underpowered 4 cylinder little car down the straight away of the oval 'track' and at just the right moment, turning into the corner and pulling on the emergency brake thereby locking up both the rear wheels, that I could actually slide around the 'track' like the big boys did in their real race cars at the fairground. OMG what fun! On my third time around the track with locked rear wheels sliding the car perfectly sideways, it was at this precise moment when the right rear wheel caught a large rock sticking out of the ground that the car went up on two wheels almost rolling over. This event even provided more enjoyment, thrill, and adventure for me. Later I found out that Uncle George happened to see this spectacular two wheel skid and almost a roll over from the side hill on his way back to the barn with the cows. However at the time I was clueless. All I saw were the cows coming down from the hill toward the barn and knew my uncle was headed for the barn, so I drove back to the side yard an parked old 144 ¼ in exactly the same spot where it had been parked over night and went in for breakfast. I was almost finished when Uncle George came in with fire in his eyes. The end result was I was banned from that hayfield with the car forever and I mean FOREVER, given a lecture on safety and the responsibility of ownership of an automobile and was told I was lucky to be alive and never to do that rear wheel emergency brake lock-up spin again. As a last painful punishment, there was to be no more 'race track' and it returned to its original status as a lowly hay field. The outline of the worn grass of the race track lasted until the first snow and the following spring there wasn't hint or trace left, only the memories.

I had old 144 ¼ parked in the side yard and was still thinking I was a race car driver; actually, I knew I was the best driver in the world! At least I thought so. What is one to do with a race car and no track? For days I worked on the car, changing the oil, cleaning the spark plugs, checking and re-gapping the points, and cleaning all the oil and grease off the engine until the paint glistened. All this time I was wondering how fast my race car would actually go. I had to wait until the perfect time. That day arrived when I was asked to stay with and play and watch the younger kids while Aunt Erma and Uncle George went to town. After they left I asked my nieces and nephew how they would like to go for a ride. Of course they were all excited about this great adventure. So we got the blankets off the beds for them to sit on since there was no back seat any more. I had a 7, a 6, and a 3 year old on a blanket on the floor of the car behind the front seat and I was a 14 year old who was going to be driving. I was not only driving, but trying to see how fast the car would go and what its top speed was. What could possibly go wrong? In the mind of a 14 year old…nothing! Cousin Dale complained he couldn't see out of the front windshield or the side windows because he was too short so we went hunting for something for him to sit on. We found it in the back storage room of the farm house. It was a copper tub used for heating water on the wood cook stove used to wash clothes in. We turned it upside down in the car, put a blanket on it and now he could now see out all of the windows and we were ready. Before taking off on our adventure everyone was told that we could not talk about this when we got back. I had a planned route so off we went, down the hardtop road to the dirt road that ran by the upper farm then down to the top of the Gulf Hill and to the hardtop and back to the farm, a total of about 7 miles. We drove carefully and slowly past the few farm houses on the macadam road so as not to arouse any notice or suspicion. Then I turned onto the dirt road and slowly, in second gear, drove up the steep hill to the top and stopped. Instructions from the driver were given and all passengers who were told to hold on tight for the run to the bottom of the hill. Slowly from a dead stop the speedometer started climbing to 25 then 40 then 55 and ever so slowly moved to 60 and we were now at the bottom of the hill. It was time to slow down and we putted our way back to the hard top and up the last hill to home. Arriving back at the farm, the car was carefully parked in the exact spot where it had been sitting before we left, blankets were quickly put away, the copper tub returned to the back room, and things returned to normal whatever that—was. Somewhere along the way that chat with Uncle George regarding the responsibility of car ownership car didn't quite sink in or, most likely, was ignored, sad to say.

I only remember Aunt Erma calling me out to the back yard that evening for THE "talk." She asked me if I knew what could have happened and made me promise I would never ever do anything like that again and especially never to involve her children. When Aunt Erma had a special talk with you, you listened intently and when you made a promise to her you would never think of breaking it. After all, Uncle George didn't ask me to promise him anything when he finished his 'talk.' I looked for an excuse any where I could find one. I now have come to believe there were angels on my shoulders that summer day. God Bless Aunt Erma for her insight, wisdom, patience, and understanding. How did she find out and know what had happened that afternoon? That is a very silly question... silly boy.

The Circus Comes to Town

It was late in the season for the second cutting of hay. As was usually the case, Uncle George was a bit behind schedule and overwhelmed with the amount of farm work left undone. As was the norm, the majority of the milk check was already promised to some creditors for previous missed payments. The 250 gallon above ground storage tank for gas for the two farm tractors had been empty for weeks and no money or credit was available to have it filled with the minimum delivery of the company's policy requirement of 100 gallons. George had to settle for Aunt Erma buying gas for the needs of the farm one five gallon can at a time.

This usually occurred when she went to town for groceries, a doctor's appointment, or to pay some long overdue and outstanding bill or a combination of all of these. George was a person who preferred staying home and seldom drove anywhere so the burden of running errands gladly fell on Erma's shoulders. If there was enough gas in the family's fifteen year- old 1939 Ford 4-door tan sedan to make it the 10 miles into town there was always the question if there was enough gas to make it back home.

If Erma could just make it six miles from the farm to the gravel pit road at the top of the hill going down into the river valley and town, she could, and usually did, turn the key off and coast down the long hill and roll right up the two gas pumps in front of Ward's Feed Store. Ward's was at the bottom of the hill leading into town on the right just after you crossed the bridge over the river and then over the double set of railroad tracks. If there was enough gas still left in the tank to restart the engine, she may have had a choice of where to buy her gas. She could drive from

Ward's a short distance into the center of the village to the other station near the town square where gas was nine-tenths of a cent cheaper per gallon. It was easy even for me to figure how much gas she could afford to buy. At a dollar fifty for five gallons at Ward's, it would cost the best part of five dollars to fill the two empty five gallon gas cans George had put in the trunk and then still be able to put just a little over five gallons in the tank of the old Ford. Five dollars was a lot of money out of the meager milk check and a huge chunk of the last lonely twenty dollar bill in Erma's wallet on this particular trip. That left her with only ten dollars for everything she needed at the grocery store and five dollars for the doctor's office visit for the baby. Ten dollars wasn't going to go very far at the A&P on this trip but that's all there was and selective shopping was always the challenge figuring out how to feed everyone and buy the needed groceries.

While Erma was in town, George was bailing hay with the big Allis Chambers WD-40 tractor using whatever gas was left in the tank and the plan for the day was that when Erma returned from town she would drive to the upper hay field to drop off two five gallon cans of gas for the tractor. If luck was on his side, George would still be bailing hay, if not; he would have run out of gas and walked home waiting to be taken back to the field with the gas cans in the trunk so he could dump it into the tractor's gas tank and be able to continue bailing the rest of the hay in the field. I had mowed this particular field and had it raked in neat twin wind rolls ready for bailing earlier that week. The hay had been drying for a few days and on this particular day it looked like it was going to rain later that afternoon or evening so this was the day to get the hay bailed up or it would have been rained on and no doubt ruined.

Erma was going to town for her errands and gas for George and she planned to take 4-year-old Thais and 2-year-old Lorna with her. Dale who was 8 years old didn't want to go and Erma asked me if I could keep him company until she returned. I readily agreed as what could be wrong with having time to hang out with your cousin for a couple of hours or more? Dale's other sister, 6-year-old Helen told her mom that she wanted to stay with the boys. Helen made a big fuss about wanting to stay and play and not wanting to ride to town and sit in the car with her two baby sisters so Erma asked me if I would look out and sort of baby sit for Helen while she was in town. It all sounded like great fun to me since I wouldn't be able to be on the tractor seat for this particular day anyhow to mow another hay field on the farm. George was in the upper hay field when Erma left with the two younger ones and headed for town in the old Ford sedan. Leaving young kids alone with older children was not an unusual occurrence in the 1950's, particularly on farms. It was an expectation that the older children would look out and take care of the younger ones while their parents were busy or working.

It was 10 in the morning when Erma left the farm and I knew it would be quite some time before she would return. I had about two hours before I had to figure out what I would make for lunch for myself as well as for Dale and Helen. Two whole hours! I thought about what we could do in that amount of time that would be the most fun and make the time fly by. It was never a problem coming up with creative and imaginary things to do and in fact, Dale and Helen always counted on this from me. I am sure that was why Helen wanted to stay with 'the boys' rather than go to town with her mom. I was not going to fail to impress my young cousins and show them a grand old time!

I was sitting on the back porch steps in deep thought trying to figure out what the play activity was going to be and how we were going to spend the morning. Helen and Dale were swinging to their hearts content on the swing set and I just kept looking out at the old barn and the new white cement block silo. As I gazed out to the barn with its missing doors, fading red paint, and missing boards, the idea hit me like a ton of bricks. The barn, that's the place to play!

It was summer and therefore the barn was almost empty of the hay and straw bales after the long winter. The bales had been used for the feeding and bedding of the cows, calves, horses, sheep and other animals. The new hay was still in the fields and the barn and hay lofts were practically empty except for the two or three feet of loose hay in the bottom of the lofts and on the main floor. George was not pleased when we played in the barn. In fact he would really rant and holler at all of us if he caught us in the barn or knew we had been in there playing in the hay. One of our favorite things to do was to climb up into the hay mows and on top of the piled bales and jump from bale to bale playing hide and seek or building huts in the hay by moving the bales around and piling them up to create little buildings or rooms in which to hide or just hang out. We called the enterprise 'building huts'. We discovered that by moving several bales that were near the front wall of the barn it was possible to slide down several feet between the bales and the wall to the attic doorway of the milk house. By removing the little door to the space above the ceiling we could actually crawl into the attic. We had to be very careful to just crawl on the 2x4 joists so as not to fall through the plaster ceiling down into the milk house itself. It was a perfect place to hide and no one could ever find us in there. Dale and I were the first to discover this hiding place. We would call out to the Dale's younger sisters and tell them to come and find us in the barn and we would then make a bee line right for the attic. The little ones would look forever trying to find us and when they grew tired of searching, we'd come out and holler again so they knew we were in the barn and in the hay loft but they couldn't find us.

George was not happy about any of us playing in the barn let alone the fact that we never bothered to put the bales back in their proper place. By all of us climbing and jumping on them they would start to come apart and the twine holding them together would unravel and they would then fall apart when George tried carrying them from the loft to the bottom of the barn to feed or bed down the animals. I know George really lost his cool with us when he found out we had been in the attic of the milk house. He was afraid we'd fall through the ceiling and if that were to have happened, the milk inspector would have refused to pick up his milk until the ceiling was repaired and then inspected again. This would no doubt have resulted in several days or weeks of being unable to ship milk and hence a loss of income and having to just dump the milk in the field. We were forbidden to ever go in the attic again and we got the message in no uncertain terms that were easily understood by every one of us kids. Even Aunt Erma could not protect us from his verbal tirade on this one. When George was angry you wanted to be sure you were a hundred miles away from him. I think his bark was much worse than his bite as I never experienced any physical punishment from him nor saw his own kids receive any, but verbal abuse can often hurt more than any spanking ever could.

So faced with the dilemma of the barn being basically off limits but being empty of hay and straw bales, how could George get upset since no bales would be ruined or moved? As for the attic crawl space in the milk house, with the bales gone the entrance to the attic was now above the floor of the loft and unreachable. Spending the next two hours in the barn while George was in the upper hay field and Erma in town and the two youngest girls not around to tattle on us, it sounded like the perfect plan. Who would ever find out if I swore Dale and Helen to secrecy? I explained the plan to both of them and they agreed not to ever say anything to anybody about us playing in the barn. Perfect plan! Let the fun begin!

Little Helen was a sweet and happy six-year-old girl and was always smiling and had a positive and bubbly personality. Almost every day her mom braided her hair into two pony tails complete with little ribbons tied to the bottom of each one before she went out to play. Girls always wore dresses in those days. Erma s mother or sister made most of the dresses for the girls. Dale and I always wore Levis. We had a good pair for Sunday and going to church or for going to the Grange Hall on Saturday night. The other pair was for everyday use along with four or five striped pull-over short sleeve shirts. On warm summer days we usually went shirtless trying to see who could get the darkest tan.

The barn had two earthen ramps leading to wide doorways on the second floor. The new cement block silo was in the center front of the barn between the ramps. Each doorway had two large sliding wooden doors that had been hung on rollers that rode on an iron rail. The sliding barn doors on the right ramp were long gone and the doorway way was open to the elements year round. The other ramp could not be used for farm equipment to enter the building so those two doors were always closed. Barn swallows flew in and out of the one open doorway as they built their mud nests. When the barn was constructed in the early 1900's, the open door way was wide enough to allow a team of horses to pull a hay wagon into the barn then be unhitched and have enough room for the team to walk out beside the hay wagon to the ramp. Once

121

out on the ramp, the horses would then be hitched to the hay rope and the hay fork that had been placed in the loose hay on the wagon to lift the hay off the wagon and move it on an iron trolley rail which ran along the entire peak of the barn. On either side where the wagon was parked, a hay loft was built to allow the loose hay to be piled in the loft almost to the peak of the barn which was twenty-four feet above the wooden plank floor. On the top of these beams were four loose beams at both the front and back walls of the barn which allowed you, if you dared to, to cross over the open floor sixteen feet below, to the other loft. There was a crude built-in ladder of sorts which allowed you to climb up the top beam of each loft.

Helen was a daredevil of a child and not afraid of heights while the same thing could not be said of either Dale or me. One time when the hay lofts had been full of bales I crawled on my hands and knees between the lofts on those loose beams that were resting loose on the top of the loft beams sixteen feet above the floor of the barn. Little Helen had no fear and just walked across the beams like she was on a balance beam at the gym following me over the other side. I didn't have the courage to crawl back and I climbed down the ladder from the other hay loft. Helen just walked back across the beam to the other side and climbed down the ladder we had first climbed up.

It made perfect sense to Dale and me that in our imagination the high beams in the barn accessible by the built-in ladder would be the center ring of the Barnum and Bailey Circus and the hay rope hanging from the very peak of the barn would be the" trapeze" rope and Helen would be the star of our circus show. As I announced the circus act, our young star would climb the ladder to the very top to the "trapeze perch" on the wooden beam, walk along the top to the end of the beam at the back wall of the barn and then, walk to the middle of the loose beams over the open part of barn above the floor and the door way in the front. Then she would grab a hold of the hay rope that was attached to the iron rail trolley at the peak. Dale was her assistant in the circus troupe and he would stand on the floor and pull the rope over so that Helen could grab it from where she was standing on the beam. She would then put the rope between her legs, hold on tight, and swing from the beam out the

122

open barn door. We had tied a large knot in the rope so Helen could sort of sit on the knot, cross her legs around the rope, hold onto the rope above to where she was sitting and swing back and forth.

"Ladieees and Genteeelmen, for your viewing pleasure, here in the center ring is young Helen the Wonder of the World and the most famous Trapeeeeezzzzs Artissssttttt the world has ever known. Watch her as she does the death defying arc on the one inch rope with no safety net beneath her. She is getting ready for the greatest performance the world has ever seen. Watch as she adjusts the rope between her legs. Watch as she locks her ankles and legs around the rope. Count with me as she prepares to swing from the perch high above your heads…10, 9, 8, 7, 6, 5, 4, 3, 2, 1……and there she goes….What a beautiful sight to watch our circus star swinging through the air!"

There were to be more circus days but they were limited to "tight rope" wooden beam walking above the circus floor although the audience wanted to see the trapeze act just one more time. The one and only circus act ended when everyone was hungry and decided to go in the old farm house for lunch where I was the renowned chef known for making the famous "Dagwood" sandwich. I made the sandwich from the available summer stock bushel of tomatoes that grandma usually brought to the farm. They sat in the back room where it was cool. I used the loaves of 'day-old' bread that the A&P supplied at a deeply discounted price. The sandwich consisted of thick sliced tomatoes smothered in mayonnaise with added salt and pepper on three toasted bread slices. Sometimes four slices were used as a challenge to see who could open wide enough to get the sandwich into their mouth for a bite. This was the staple lunch all through tomato season and we all loved them and never tired of them. And so the day 'the circus came to town' may have been the only secret my Aunt and Uncle never knew about… or perhaps NOT?

Return of the Circus

After lunch what better thing to do on a warm summer day than to move the circus act out-of-doors? We checked the clock in the kitchen and it was 12:15. We figured we had at least two more hours alone and on our own. Dale and I decided, or maybe better stated, I suggested to Dale that our next greatest Barnum and Bailey Circus act take place center ring with a tree instead of trapeze. No tight rope was required for this act and it had to be a bit safer than the last circus act. After all, there was no chance of Helen hitting the beam on the side of barn door opening on a swinging rope. We had heard stories of a horse in a circus diving into a pool from a high perch, a circus performer diving 30 feet into a five foot pool of water, and trapeze artists letting go at the end of their act and falling into a net. What could be simpler than to design and have a greater act than all three of these? That was the concept and that was the plan. Little Helen, our own world-renowned circus star, would climb up a tall white birch tree to the very top branches and 'ride' it all the way down to the ground of the 'center ring' of the 'circus.' What a grand idea! Helen was all set for trying it.

Dale and I had experience in chopping trees down with an axe to build our fort. Our experience with tall birch trees we had used indicated that it seemed to take a few seconds for them to topple and fall to the ground. The trees that we cut fell slowly in almost what seemed to be in slow motion. When they landed, protected by branches as they hit the ground first, they seemed to fall softly before the main trunk of the tree hit the ground. With these observations and our experience behind us we figured this was a 'safe' plan for Helen and she wouldn't get hurt. We prepared for the second greatest circus act that the world had ever seen! Our young artist seemed more than ready and willing to perform this feat after both Dale and I told her that she would be safe as the tree would come down slowly and land softly. After being assured by both her older brother and me that it would be a slow "ride" to the ground with a soft landing and most importantly, it would be FUN, Helen couldn't wait to be the circus star once again. The three of us were off with the axe to find the perfect tree for the second circus act. What a brilliant plan we had devised!

I picked up the long handle double bladed axe from the wood pile and the three of us walked to the barn, climbed the wooden fence leading to the cattle path and followed it to the end of the pond. We crossed the earthen dam and climbed the side hill to the stand of birch trees growing by the stone foundation of where the old hay barn once stood. The perfect tree was selected not only for its height but also for the number of branches it had that were close together and would make it easier for Helen to climb. Dale and I took turns chopping. The axe was very sharp and it took big chunks of wood out of the tree with each swing. We were careful to notch the tree so we could direct its journey to the ground to a spot we had hoped it would fall. We wanted the tree to fall uphill rather than downhill so it would be a shorter distance to the ground. We notched the tree on the uphill side and began chopping just above the notch. When the tree was almost cut through all the way and we could make it move by just pushing on it above the notch, the circus announcer exclaimed, "Ladieees and Genteeelmen, here in our center ring is the world's greatest circus performer, Little Helen, doing her death defying tree ride all the way to the ground."

Dale was given the signal to take a few more swings of the axe and slowly the tree began to fall in the right direction, uphill! The white birch was very tall and about six inches around in diameter at its base. Our star circus artist and performer had an exciting and supreme 'ride' all the way down to the ground accompanied by the sound of both Dale and I shouting "timber". Helen was on the right side of the tree when it fell, that is, landing on the top side of the tree and not the ground side. The branches softened the tree as it toppled and the light weight of

Helen didn't seem to make any difference in the swiftness of its descent. Helen did not even receive a scratch or bruise. No broken arms, legs, or cracked skull. Unbelievable and looking back at this event, a blessing! It is to our star performer's credit that she moved quickly around the tree from one side to the other as it began to fall. Helen was like a monkey scrambling from branch to branch as the tree was starting to fall so as to be on the right side, that is the top side of the tree as it was on it trajectory path to the ground. At the moment the last cut of the axe had been delivered I was very scared as I, for the first time it seemed, realized what might happen to her with this ill conceived stunt. I began shouting to her to move quickly and get to the other side of the tree! She did and she made it!

After this performance everyone was sworn to secrecy and we all knew that we could not breathe a work of this circus act that had just been performed to anyone. This was the greatest circus act in the history of the world! As for our artist, she remembers a bit of her performance even to this day as I try as best I can to erase it from my memory. As the years have slowly drifted by I feel we were all blessed and I know an angel was sitting on Helen's shoulder as she made her descent to the ground. I shudder to think what could have happened with either one of these 'performances.' Maybe on this day God was smiling down on us. How will we ever know? I think I already have the answer the answer…

Allis

The Allis-Chalmers model C was a wonderful machine. As a 12-year-old it was my ship to command and control. I was its captain. It was power at my finger tips. Never mind it was just a tractor... it was my entrance in to the world of adulthood, at least in my mind.

My introduction to the Allis-Chalmers was watching Aunt Erma bouncing around on the seat of the tractor dragging a set of disks behind going around and around the 18 acre field next to the old farm house. My task was to play with Cousin Dale in the front and side yards while Erma worked the field to get it ready for planting. Every 10 or 15 trips she would drive up in the field near the side porch and either get off to check on us or to get a glass of water. After a couple of hours she would drive up in the field near the porch and shut off the engine and climb down. Then we knew it was lunch time. Usually we had what we called a "picnic" which consisted of a blanket being spread on the old boards of the floor of the side porch and a lunch of thick sandwiches of peanut butter and home-made strawberry jam along with Kool-Aid made with extra sugar for a special sweet taste.

My second introduction to the Allis was in the dead of winter during Christmas vacation from school when we visited the farm for the holidays. Uncle George had the tractor hooked up to a buzz saw which consisted of having it backed up to the saw about 10 feet away and connected via a wide canvas-rubber belt from the pulley on the back of the tractor which was under the seat to the pulley on the end of the shaft of the buzz saw. On the other end of the shaft of the saw was a huge round saw blade about 3 feet in diameter. My Uncle would first crank the tractor engine to get it started and then climb up on the tractor; push the clutch in and at the same time reach down and pull up a lever under the seat to engage the rear pulley of the tractor while slowly letting the clutch pedal out. Then the big saw blade would start turning and soon it was at full speed and the high pitch blade spinning in the air would almost drown out the sound of the engine. Uncle George would then walk back to the saw and lift a large trimmed tree branch or log up and onto the table and position the piece of wood to the right length and slowly push the table forward moving the log into the spinning blade. Wood chips and saw dust would fly filling the air and covering George's hat, jacket, and pants with tiny particles of wood and the end of the log would fall to the ground. Soon a pile of wood chips and saw dust would grow under the blade along with the pile of cut off pieces of wood.

George would then walk over to the tractor, reach in and push the lever down and take the power-take off out of gear and the whirling saw blade would slowly come to a stop and the pile of wood would be cleared away from the blade so room could be made for more cut offs to pile up. Uncle George was emphatic that this was a most dangerous mechanical device on the farm that he owned and that he and I had to be very careful not to get near the spinning blade or the belt and even more careful not to trip on a piece of wood or a log and fall into the blade or onto the belt. He made a point to tell me about farmers he knew who tripped and fell on the belt had their hands or arms ripped off after being caught on the belt or just having their glove, jacket sleeve, or pant leg caught in the belt or pulley. He also shared stories complete with all the gory details of how farmers he knew had tripped on a log or piece of wood and had fallen into the blade having their hand, arm or even their head cut off buy the spinning blade. Other accident stories included one where the farmer's chest was cut open just like the hunter who would open the chest of a deer he shot to "gut it." Whatever the intent of these tales, they worked, as I never ventured close to that buzz saw, whether it was spinning or not or even if wasn't hooked to the tractor. I was even scared to fetch wood from that wood pile to bring it into the house when Aunt Erma told me she needed it for the kitchen stove and for the stove in the front room of the house called the "play room." It was most important to have wood for the pot belly stove in the play room because that is where the model train was set up at Christmas time for Dale and me to play with and who knew what Santa might bring on Christmas morning to be added to the train "set-up"? Filling the wood box in the "back room" was not a problem with this kind of motivated thinking when being asked to complete this task. That wood box would be filled during the whole of Christmas vacation.

My third introduction to Allis was when Uncle George attached "mowing machine" to the undercarriage of the tractor at the beginning of my summer vacation on the farm. Then I watched as he gave instructions to Aunt Erma at the edge of the same 18 acre field she had dragged with the discs the summer before. From my vantage point standing on the porch with Dale during the period of instruction and then watching the actual mowing down of the hay as the Allis went round and round on the outer edge of the field, I thought, I can do that. It's easy.

And so it came to be that Aunt Erma was going to have another baby and was "too big" to drive the tractor because the steering wheel hit her belly that I suggested to Uncle George that I could cut the hay in the field. I recall the many discussions my Aunt and Uncle had privately that I over-heard about how dangerous the tractor was, but how much I was interested and how old I was and how big I was and back to how dangerous it was to drive the tractor and to operate the mowing attachment with the moving cutting blades. Given the complex combination of the new baby on the way, my interest in driving the tractor, the amount of work to do on the farm, the nice weather before the rain comes, the hay already cut which needed bailing, and not enough time to do everything, and a decision was made. Given safety instructions first, the test was that if I could start the tractor by myself, operate the mower and drive straight in the field for mowing and take the cutting blade off the machine by myself, sharpen it correctly, I might be allowed to use the tractor to cut hay.

The safety instructions included, among other things: never get off the tractor with the engine running and always have it in gear and the brakes on and locked before getting off, watch for rocks and stones in the field and never let the mowing blade hit one, and don't mow with a dull blade and never leave any hay standing especially at the corners of each pass or turn. The safety instructional talk was complete with vivid and graphic descriptions of farmers who got off their tractors with the engine left running and how they had a foot cut off at the ankle when the tractor rolled forward or how they reached down to remove a rock only to have a hand cut off by the moving blades. It worked! I wasn't even sure that if I passed all these tests if I now wanted to mow hay and drive the tractor. To this day I am still afraid to use a table saw or hand saw to cut a piece of wood. I can and do but I am so very careful. The safety instructions worked!

The test began. Get on the tractor and make sure it is in neutral and then set the brakes. Get off and turn the gas on for the carburetor, turn on the choke, crank the tractor to start it and crank it the right way, that is hold your thumb to the outside of the handle so you won't have it broken if the engine back fires, get the engine started, and then quickly run and push the choke in. I passed that part. Next, use the correct tools to undo the bolts, remove the 5 foot cutting bar, carry it to the barn and to the grinding wheel, grind each side of each tooth perfectly to the sharpest possible cutting edge, carry it back to the tractor, reassemble and properly tighten the bolts. I passed that test also! It was now time for the real test. Drive to the field with Uncle George aboard, make a perfect cut on all four sides of the field paying particular attention to the corner cuts and leave no hay standing. I passed that one also. And finally the field was mine. And so on that glorious day I cut the remaining standing hay in the 18-acre-field. I was captain of my own ship!

Guess what? After hay is cut it is left to dry for a day or two but then it has to be raked then bailed and finally picked up and taken to the barn. I only accomplished a quarter of the job and it had taken me all day. The safety instruction for raking came next. I was told about a farmer who fell off the tractor and was run over by the rake and left in the wind row only to be found dead by his wife who went searching for him when he was not home in time to milk the cows and have supper. OK, I'm set, I won't, no matter what happens, fall off the tractor even if I get hit with a tree while driving under it at the edge of the field or by not looking forward once in a while looking backwards to make sure my wind rows are perfectly set for bailing. I secured my place as captain of my ship once again as Uncle George raved about my perfect wind rows that were just right for bailing. My Uncle wisely thought that all the bailing should be done by his hand but he would show me how it was done. And so he did. I was glad he did the bailing as I watched the mechanical difficulties encountered with the process and the repairs and adjustments to the bailing machine that needed to be made in the field. I was left to do all the mowing and raking I wanted and to spend as many hours on the Allis-Chalmers that I cared to. At this point in my life I knew I wanted to be a farmer and drive a tractor for the rest of my life. What more to being a farmer could there be? And as I grew older, I was sure I could master bailing hay just as I had mastered mowing and raking. I thought that life was so simple and I'd make a great farmer!

Camping on the River Bottom

I made some new friends at summer Bible School in the Town of Cameron Mills. They were boys who were about my age, from a large family and they had a sister also, maybe a little younger, maybe a little older, hard to tell when you are not focused on the important details. I figured that the sister could be a plus since I was just beginning to be interested in girls. I wasn't quite sure about them at this juncture in my unfolding life's plans. That being the case, I received an invitation to spend a couple of days with them at their house after the week of Bible School ended. I posed this idea to Aunt Erma and I figured somehow she'd check it out. She did, but how, I don't know. But then, when you think about it, everyone knew everyone in the small rural communities in the 1950's. I don't remember all the details or even how it all came to pass, but the issue became how I was going to get over to and back from the boys' home which was 15 miles away. I think I was so in love with driving Miss Allis I may have suggested that I could drive the tractor over to their house. It was a far-out crazy impossible dream of an idea not based in reality. I even realized that at the time I made the suggestion.

The next day, Aunt Erma informed me that she and Uncle George would allow me to drive the tractor, Miss Allis, over to the boys' house if I were very careful and took the back dirt roads. Having no sense of direction, Aunt Erma even drew me a map to follow to get to the house. Final instructions were given and I was off on this great adventure. I'm fairly sure this journey was approved for all the seat time I spent cutting and raking hay this particular summer. I'd guess that morning summer Bible School for the week didn't interfere with getting all the mowing and raking done that needed to be accomplished. I do remember going to Bible School each day for the week it was held and being picked up in and delivered back to the farm in a rickety old used former school bus now called the church bus. After returning back to the farm at lunch time and a quick bite to eat, I was back on Miss Allis working in the hay fields.

So off I went for my two day adventure. Little did I know or expect to be unsupervised. The boys and this family were a wild bunch. I thought I was pretty wild myself but I wasn't prepared for things that were about to unfold. First, upon arrival, I was escorted to the kitchen for something to eat. Help yourself, make a sandwich. "Oh, this is my mother," was the introduction. We were then left to fend for ourselves which I had no problem doing as I had much prior experience and practice.

After "lunch" it was off to explore the recently abandoned one room school house which was a long walk up the dirt road from the farm where I was going to spend the next two days. After arriving, I asked how we were going to get in. "Simple," I was told, "We'd break in." And so we did by pulling nailed boards off a back window, lifting the window up and crawling in. Once inside I looked around and saw it was complete with desks, blackboards, teacher's desk, stove, buckets, a piano, and even neat stacks of books in a cupboard. My new friends allowed me to look through the books. I was fascinated with all of them. They wanted to throw them around the room and I told them we did not want to do that because our fingerprints would be on the books and we could get caught. I suggested we draw pictures on the blackboard instead. We hunted around and found a few bits of chalk and I was educated by two farm boys about dirty pictures. I wasn't quite ready for this type of art work and suggested we leave. It helped cement the deal when we heard a car coming down the hill on the dirt road. We became very quiet and listened carefully to see if it was going to stop. It didn't and we left quickly after it passed.

Back at the house later that afternoon I was asked if I had ever fired a .22 rifle. I told them I had, which was true. The boys then decided that we should have a target shooting contest. First we started with tin cans on the fence posts behind the barn. Then we progressed to glass bottles for a more explosive reaction. Tin cans just fall off the posts but glass bottles explode! After shooting and breaking every glass bottle we could find, the boys decided to find out who was the best marksman among the three of us. The contest was developed around the concept of accurate shooting by placing a 12 gauge shotgun shell on the top of a fence post. The object was to hit the primer in the brass end of the shell with the .22 caliber bullet. There would be no doubt as to who the winner would be because the shotgun shell would explode if hit by the .22 bullet. Every time it was my turn I was sure to aim at the fence post and not the shotgun shell. This is one contest I did not want to win. We all missed several times… maybe they were also aiming at the fence post.

Dinner was nondescript and unmemorable… as I remember. It was decided that we would camp out and sleep on the banks of the river. The river was about a mile away from the farm. We camped at what the boys referred to as the "river bottom." The bothers invited their sister to go with us which was fine with me. Our camping gear consisted of magazine, a pack of matches, 2 blankets each, a frying pan, a pot, fishing poles, and "goodie bag" we filled from the kitchen pantry. The goodie bag held a three cans of Campbell's pork and beans, a bag of marshmallows, a box of Saltine crackers, and a jar of peanut butter. We each had our own jack knives to open the cans and a blade to spread the peanut butter. We were traveling light as our plan was to have fresh fish for supper.

We spent time before fishing by skipping stones on the water. After trying to find some worms for bait and not having much luck at all we had the brilliant idea to go to the woods to find old rotten logs on the ground and to roll them over and gather grubs which make for great fish bait. After a long hike to the woods we were successful in finding a few grubs and then we trudged back to the river bottom. Sister Sue was waiting for us completely bored out of her mind and pretty much unimpressed with our success at finding them. She was even less impressed with what they looked like.

After what seemed like hours fishing and having no luck and with sunlight fading and dusk coming quickly, we were a hungry bunch. We decided it was time to collect wood and start a fire. Sister Sue was hungry and even more unimpressed with her brothers and their "city boy" guest. A roaring fire provided some warmth and hot pork and beans followed by toasted marshmallows on a stick. The pork and beans were served by passing around the pot and the one spoon we brought with us. The spoon also served as a knife for the peanut butter as our jack knife blades were sharp and not as long as the handle of the spoon. Sister Sue refused to eat using only the one spoon by sharing it. After the marshmallows were gone it was time to enjoy the Saltines and peanut butter. They were gone in a flash. Soon everyone realized they were thirsty but no one had thought to bring anything to drink. We were off to the river with a dirty pot and a spoon to wash and we returned with a pot full of water and wet feet. Sister Sue refused to drink the water and left us to our own devices to walk home alone and get something to drink. We snuggled in our blankets as close to the fire as possible laying on the stones and pebbles of the riverbed. The three of us were cold and hungry with wet feet and we decided we had enough of camping and headed for the farm house a short while after Sister Sue left. When we arrived the boys went upstairs to bed and I was assigned the sofa for the duration of the evening. I still had wet feet and the two damp and dirty blankets for a cover. Sleep came quickly and soon it was morning.

Breakfast was a free for all. First off to the barn to find chicken nests for some eggs and back to the kitchen to fry 'em. We made stacks of toast and fried the eggs and a few pieces of bacon we found in the refrigerator. The boys made coffee for themselves and offered it to me. I had no desire to drink it as I didn't like the taste of it. Over breakfast we talked about tractors. The boys bragged and bragged about how powerful their Farmall tractor was. I was skeptical about the tales being told and we decided to have a tractor pulling contest. By the way, this is a very dangerous thing to do. We hooked the two tractors together with a heavy log chain and the Allis pulled that Farmall backwards 3 out of 3. Truth be told, it wasn't so much about horse power; it was more about new tires on the Allis-Chalmers and the old worn out tires on the Farmall which couldn't get a grip in the dirt and grass.

The next morning I left for Uncle George's and Aunt Erma's and had a peaceful and wonderful ride back. That evening over dinner they were most anxious to find out what we did and what kind of a time I had. I mentioned we did some target shooting but didn't mention the cans and glass bottles and for sure didn't say a word about the trip to the old one room school. I told them about our camping trip and somehow slipped up telling about how powerful the AC tractor was. My Uncle became very interested in that comment and eventually it all came out. I listened intently to the safety lecture and the danger in doing what we did but I'm sure I noted a small smile on Uncle George's lips when I was telling about pulling that Farmall tractor backwards 3 out of 3 times.

The Little AC Tractor

As I was preparing for 'helping out' this particular week I had
to hitch-hike to town with the five dollars which my mother
had given me for spending money at the beginning of my
summer vacation. I was off to purchase fuel for the tractor. I knew I
needed a dollar and a half to fill the five gallon gas can in my hand so I
would have gas for the tractor in order to mow the hay field. A ride was
fairly easy to come by if, and this was always the big if, if a car or truck
was on the road traveling to town for some reason. There was very little
traffic on County Route 10 where the farm was located and almost
anyone driving into town using the road was from a neighboring farm or
one of the farms on the dirt roads off this narrow macadam County road.
It was really a one lane paved road and so narrow that when meeting on-
coming traffic both vehicles had to have two of their wheels off the paved
portion and on the gravel shoulder of the road. Since there was precious
little traffic, I would start out walking towards town 10 miles away until
I heard a vehicle coming and then turn around and walking backwards,
face the car or truck and stick my thumb out. On a hot summer day with
all the time in the world to make it into town and back again, it was a
wonderful adventure.

Well... most of the time it was enjoyable except the one time
returning to the farm with a full five gallon can of gas and I had to walk
two miles from town up the long hill towards the gravel pit road before
a car came along and I was able to hitch a ride to the bottom of what the
locals called the Gulf Hill. At this intersection the driver had to turn off
to go to his farm. I was still a long mile from the farm and it was up hill
almost the entire way until I reached Uncle George's sister's farm and

Aunt Margie's house. Then the road leveled out and it was a short walk to the farm which was the next one up the road. For a 14 year old, a full five gallon gas can gets very heavy fairly quickly and I felt my arms were like huge rubber bands being slowly stretched by a couple of inches with each half-hour passing by as I walked up the steep hill. If I could just hold the handle of the can and let my arm stretch out, the can would touch and drag on the ground so to carry the can I had to actually do a bit of an arm curl to lift it higher to clear the shoulder of the road where I was walking. This resulted in many required rest stops about every 100 feet or so. It also resulted in slow progress and made for a very time consuming trip. An unexpected added benefit was that I developed exceptional upper body strength that summer which was a huge plus as a freshman wrestler that fall when I returned to school.

I finally had made it back to the farm. The little orange Allis-Chambers model C tractor with the mowing attachment on it, sat in the side yard by the farm house. I struggled to lift the can up to the opening on the gas tank on the top of the tractor. When I got it up to the tank I had to turn the can upside down in order to pour the gas out and into the tank. This maneuver turned out to be a real feat to accomplish successfully without spilling fuel all over the tractor and myself. There were two screw caps on the old style gas cans, a large one about the size of a half-dollar and a smaller one built on top of the larger one with the opening about the size of a dime. You could remove the large top as a unit and the smaller top came off with it or you could just remove the smaller cap. The small one was designed to pour gas into a tank of a lawn mower or chain saw. I could not remove the large top and turn the can upside down to pour the gas into the tank without spilling a lot of the gas all over the tractor, the ground, and myself. The only choice I had was to unscrew the small cap, put the tip of my index finger over the dime sized hole, turn the can upside down and insert the nozzle into the tank with my figure on the end and then try to remove my finger with the full weight of the can and five gallons of gas pressing on that finger while it was being pinched between the snout of the can and the rim of the gas tank. While I was executing this maneuver I was remembering the day I just spent going to town to get the gas and not wanting to spill a precious drop. These last thoughts made the pain somewhat bearable. It was the end result which drove me to accomplish this almost impossible feat and that was to have gas in the tank so I could climb up on the seat and spend more time on the tractor. These five gallons would allow me about five hours of mowing time including driving up to the upper hay field and returning back to the farm house. All this and a sore index finger just to spend some seat time on the little AC tractor. Was it worth it? You bet it was!

Damn Fools

A rmy Surplus Stores were commonplace in almost every city during the decade following WWII. I loved walking through these places searching for bargain prices on high quality merchandise. It was the perfect place for the creative and the mechanically inclined to find intriguing items and try to figure out how these items could be used or modified for other applications than what they had been designed for. It was a wonderful experience to wander through these stores and find interesting gadgets, equipment, tools, gauges, and the most unusual new as well as used military items.

While I was still in high school my friend George and I found a Navy survival suit in one of these stores. It was a full black rubber garment with a zipper that ran up the front from the groin area to the neck. You had to work your feet into the legs of the suit and down into the boots which were part of the one piece suit. Then you worked your hands and arms into the sleeves and down into the attached thick rubber gloves. At this point it became a two person operation to finish suiting up since the other person had to then pull the top of the suit up and over your head and around your face covering all your hair as well as your ears and all that was left was a small round oval portion of your face showing . Your partner then had to zip up the front and you were in an insulated waterproof full body rubber sea rescue survival suit. There was a small rubber hose attached to the suit and the other end was near your mouth on the shoulder of the suit. We quickly figured out that you could open the valve and blow air into the tube to inflate the suit which was designed to provide Navy seamen with a layer of air between their body and the rubber skin of the suit to protect them from cold ocean water. The rubber suit being so tight around your face and with no other openings, held in the air and you could 'blow' yourself up to be almost twice your normal size. We pooled our money and bought the suit and discovered all these great tricks and how it worked after we got it home, unrolled it, and tried it out.

The next thing we thought of was that perhaps with this suit on we could float in water since it held air when you blew it up, but we had to test this theory out to be sure it worked the way we envisioned. We thought the best and safest test site would be to try it out at Aunt Erma and Uncle George's farm because there was a very large pond down the hill and behind the barn. The water in the pond covered several acres of land, was spring fed, and it was deep as well as cold.

My buddy George and I arrived at the farm early one Saturday morning after driving down from the city. I checked in with Aunt Erma for her approval and her blessing for our mission. I assisted in getting George into the suit while we were on the bank of the pond and told him to slowly wade in. All the time he was wading in he was blowing air into the suit and he was starting to look like the Pillsbury Dough Boy but with his arms sticking out like a scarecrow. As he waded into the deeper water he started to float to the point that he was bobbing up and down in the water and was having a difficult time keeping his feet and legs down and his head pointed in the right direction to breathe air instead of H_2O. The suit had so much air in it that it wanted to float horizontal rather than vertical. Now this is not a problem if you wind up floating on your back but things were not working out in George's favor. We quickly figured that whatever laws of physics were operational here, George was in a heap of trouble floating with his face in the water and drifting along like a bobber on a fish line.

Timing is everything. While my friend George was in the water trying to get right side up as well as trying to get to shore to stand up, Uncle George came out of the barn after he had just finished his milking chores and was headed to the house for breakfast. He must have heard us yelling at each other down at the pond and he came running down the hill. I think the lecture ended with something like, "...you damn fools." Perhaps the language was even a bit more colorful than even that!

141

Damn fools we may have been that weekend but Halloween was fast approaching and we had a new and better plan that didn't involve a near drowning! In fact, it had nothing to do with water what so ever as we knew we were better suited for dry land maneuvers on land rather than water. On Halloween eve I managed to get the suit on George and get him into his car behind the steering wheel before he began adding air in the tube and inflating it. He kept blowing in the tube and expanding the suit that he was so huge that he had difficulty turning the steering wheel with the seat pushed all the way back. He looked so enormous life form from outer space with a little oval face with two eyes and a nose showing. It was a great Halloween for both of us that year driving around the city in that black rubber suit and waving at everyone and blowing the horn to get everyone's attention. We did stop traffic more than once and we did not get caught or stopped by the police, even after driving down Main Street, stopping in the middle of traffic, getting out, running around the car and getting back in and driving off. What a great Halloween prank and I'm sure that if Uncle George knew what we did he'd say more than, "… you damn fools."

A Very Bad Day

It was a bad day for the Allis-Chalmers model C tractor... a very bad day. I decided that even if there was real work connected in any way that would allow me to be on the tractor, then that was a good thing. Toward the end of one of my summer vacations on the farm and after all the hay had been cut, racked and bailed, most of it still was in the fields. Other chores and farm tasks didn't allow time for Uncle George to pick up the bales and take them to the barn and load them into the hay loft. For a youngster my age, there was a bit of work involved in doing this because it was a one person operation where normally it would require two, one to drive the tractor and one to load the bales on the wagon. Doing this alone involved driving between two rows of bales, stopping the tractor, getting off, loading the bales on the wagon, and then driving a bit further in the field and continuing the process.

When stopped, I had to walk back and pick up a bale weighing 50-70 pounds, carry it back to the wagon, toss it on and in a proper place, walking to pick up the next bale and repeating this on both rows of bales on each side of the wagon until it was too far to walk carrying the bale and it made sense to climb back on the tractor and drive it forward until I was closer to the next cluster of bales. So a lot of walking, carrying, and climbing on and off the tractor was involved. To further complicate this task and add to the work load, the bales had to be placed on the wagon correctly so as to have a full load. The round bales had to be lifted 3 feet onto the wagon and placed at a 90 degree angle to the floor of the wagon. This way, there would be 3 rolls on the wagon bed. One row was placed in the middle with a roll down each side. So the first row to be filled was the middle which required that after placing the number of bales needed for the length of the row, I had to jump up on the wagon and drag each one of the bales into the middle to allow the placement of bales on each side next to the middle row. The first layer was fairly easy but when it came time to do the second row, I now had the 3 feet off the ground to lift the bale plus an additional 2 feet higher given the diameter of the first row of bales to get it up far enough to make the second row. Each additional row added another 2 feet to the height I had to lift the bale. So, for the higher rows, I had to carry the bale to the wagon, turn it vertical, lift it by its end and then push it up and onto the highest layer of bales. The wagon was fully loaded when I could fully extend my arms above my head and tip the bale onto the top of the load. For every row, I had to climb up onto the wagon and drag the bales and place them in the center. This was the task for getting a load of bales from the field.

Regarding the operation cycle for moving the tractor, I would climb up on the tractor, drive forward, set the brakes, and then get back off to pick up bales. On the fateful day, I had the third layer of bales on the wagon and I was getting very tired. The tractor and wagon was on the steeper side of the hay field and I set the brakes, jumped off, and started walking back to pick up the furthest bale from the wagon. When I reached the bale, picked it up and turned towards the wagon, the tractor and wagon was slowly inching forward and rolling down the hill. The brakes probably were not fully set. I dropped the bale and started running back toward the tractor. The tractor with its heavy load of hay was gaining momentum. As it was gaining speed and moving faster I first thought that I could catch up to the tractor, jump on, apply the brakes and simply steer it up hill and it would stop. My second thought was, given the rate of acceleration, was I was going to get run over and killed trying to climb on. I didn't think that was a good idea so I stopped dead in my tracks and watched the tractor and wagon rolling out of control down the field toward the road.

Oh, how I wished that the tractor somehow would turn itself and change direction away from the road. This was wishful thinking on my part but to no avail. As I stood there watching all of this unfold before my very eyes, the first thing I saw was the tractor going over the steep bank above the road and disappear from sight. Then I saw the wagon disappear because of the steep bank and drop off to the road. The next most amazing thing I saw was that both of the rear wheels reappear without being attached to the tractor and they were rolling by themselves up the furthest side bank of the roadway. I stood there in disbelief. Then I started to run down the hill toward the road. When I got to the point where I could see the road, there sat the tractor without any rear wheels or tires right in the middle of the road with the wagon still attached with half of the hay bales on it and the other half of the bales all over the road. It was a bad day for the Allis-Chalmers model C tractor, a very bad day. And I feared it was going to be a very bad day for me also.

With the tractor blocking the road and traffic stopped someone called the Sheriff. I didn't know about this until later because as I saw the wrecked tractor in the road I took off running across the fields and down the side hill to the farm house to tell Aunt Erma and Uncle George what had happened. I was out of breath and between tears and gasping for air, I blurted out my story of woe to Erma. I think she thought I was dramatizing the incident when I told her about the tractor having no rear wheels and just sitting in the road. She said it couldn't be THAT bad! I told her it was totally ruined. Totally! She listened, told me not to worry and to stop crying and she would tell Uncle George when he got home. It seemed like hours of waiting and I'm sure it was. It turned out that the Sheriff contacted George and he was at the scene of the disaster making arrangements to have the tractor, wagon, and hay bales cleared from the highway. Since the roadway was shut down until it was cleared, word spread around "Farmville" very quickly.

Uncle George arrived home late for supper and Aunt Erma told him what I had told her. I just knew I was as good as dead as I knew Uncle George was going to kill me right then and there. But an amazing thing happened. Both he and my Aunt were just happy that I was safe and wasn't hurt. My Uncle George told me not to worry because the tractor needed to be refurbished anyway and this was as good a time as any to send it to the garage for repair. I think they both were relieved that I didn't try to get back on the tractor as it was rolling out of control through the hay field. When I arrived for my Christmas vacation on the farm that year I saw a newly painted orange Allis-Chalmers sitting by the barn. Later in the day when I saw uncle George he asked me if he thought I could take the tractor and wagon the next day and get big load of wood for the stove to save him some time. He didn't even give me a safety lecture! All he said the next morning was that it was very cold and that I might have a hard time starting the tractor and to leave the choke on a bit longer than usual. But he did tell me to remember how to hold the crank and my thumb so I wouldn't break it or my wrist because I would not be able to write when I went back to school. He trusted me with the tractor and gave me a second chance to prove that I could use good judgment and be responsible. Go figure...

Gravity Can Be a Friend or Foe

Gravity can provide wonderful assistance when searching for speed. As you are planning a wild wagon ride it is an absolute necessary. The idea for a wild ride was hatched when we found the old horse drawn abandoned manure spreader up on the big steep side hill near the stone foundation where the hay barn had been built years before. The manure wagon had huge rear steel spoke wheels with smaller ones in the front. The tongue to the wagon used to tow it by a team of horses was long gone and the front wheels were left to point in any random direction. The wagon had a wooden floor with sides bolted to upright steel posts and to the frame. The floor also had chains running along both sides with angle iron pieces placed about a foot apart and this apparatus would move along the floor of the wagon driven by the turning of the rear wheels as it moved thus moving the load of manure towards the back of the machine when it was being pulled by horses. At the very back of the spreader were spinning steel forks and tangs that were also driven by the rear wheels when the wagon moving and was in gear. These spinning forks and tangs would dig into the pile of manure as it was carried rearward by the slowly moving chains cross bars on the floor. All of these mechanical movements were controlled by gear shift handles at the front of the machine near the seat where the operator would sit. In its current state of abandonment, the seat was missing.

We had our star daredevil from our circus shows. It did not take much salesmanship to convince our star performer to ride the wagon down the hill for about a quarter of a mile. We promised Helen a fun ride that would be better than anything on the midway at the Bath

County Fair. Our star was a bit concerned about the fence at the bottom where the slope of the hill leveled out. She was also hesitant about the large body of water beyond the fence as she did not want to get her dress wet. I was the ring master and my assistant was Dale, Helen's brother. We both assured her that the wagon would come to a stop well before the fence and of course since it would coast to a stop before it got to the fence there was no way she would get wet. Just in case we miscalculated we figured that the fence would be a safety net and act as barrier to stop the wagon. With these assurances, the plan was approved by Helen and now we were ready to set it into action.

First things first, the positioning of the wagon was critical. We had to move a one ton manure spreader wagon into position facing downhill without it taking off and rolling down the hill by itself before getting Helen aboard and in position. Since the wagon was sitting sideways on the hill in a parked position we had to get it moved and headed downhill. We accomplished this by grabbing the spokes on one rear wheel and Dale doing the same on the opposite wheel while Helen's job was to turn the front wheels in the right direction. Then Dale and I heaved our guts out pulling on the spokes and even climbing on them to move the wagon. By moving it a little bit at a time and blocking the rear wheels with big stones we were able to prevent it from rolling down the hill by itself. After an hour or two of difficult physical effort, we were able to get it into position and pointed downhill.

We got the star of the show into the wagon. We supervised her and told her to carefully sit in the middle on the wooden floor between the angle iron scraper bars. Instructions were given to hold on tight to both sides of the wagon and do not get near the spines and iron spikes and tangs of the spreader bars at the back because they would hurt. The shifting levers were checked to make sure they were in neutral and that the rear wheels would not drive the floor scraper bars or the bars with the spikes and tangs on them. Assurances were given to Helen that the wagon would go straight down the hill and come to a stop on the level ground well before reaching the fence. Additionally we assured her that just in case something did go wrong, which would not happen, the fence would be the safety net and will stop the machine before it could roll into the water. Helen was only worried about getting her dress or shoes wet or muddy. We assured her that would not happen. The excitement was building and I, as the master of ceremonies, announced that the world's greatest wild wagon ride was about to take place.

The stones in front of the rear wheels were removed. First the right one and then with the pry of a tree branch, the left stone was loosened and pulled out of the way. The wagon slowly starting moving forward and all of a sudden the laws of physics took over and the wagon picked up speed and then faster and faster it was rolling, careening, bucking, shaking, and wobbling front to back and side to side going down the steep side hill. Our star performer was holding on tight but was bouncing up and down off the wooded floor like a ping pong ball dropped from a great height on a cement floor. As the speed built up on the descent, the now wild beast of a machine somehow managed to go in a straight line even with no steering mechanism in place. In a matter of seconds the wagon was on almost level ground but the speed did not seem to diminish very much and the fence was getting closer and closer.

Then the unbelievable happened. At what seemed to be full speed the contraption went through the barbwire fence pulling out the fence posts attached to the three stands of wire. The beast continued on into the water with wire and fence posts attached at the front and finally settled into the muddy bottom of the pond in three feet of water just perfectly so that our star performer did not even get wet where she was sitting. Dale and I were running down the hill to catch up with the beast and we told Helen to just walk to the back of the manure spreader near the metal spreader bars. I took off my shoes and pants and walked into the water and picked up Helen and carried her back to dry ground. I said, "Helen, wasn't that a lot of fun I?" She agreed..."That was a lot of fun!"

There was no way we could turn the spokes on the back wheels by hand to even move the spreader an inch. It had sunk in the mud at the pond's bottom. When Uncle George discovered the situation we were questioned about how and why this happened. I think we came up with the story that the three of us were playing with the old manure spreader up on the side hill and somehow it started rolling down the hill. No mention was ever made about the fact that there was a passenger in it when it rolled down the hill. Both Uncle George and Aunt Erma praised us for getting out of the way when it started to roll and not trying to stop it because we could have been seriously injured or even killed. All three of us felt like heroes that day. God works in mysterious ways!

In an Instant

After committing these stories to a manuscript, I took a road trip in my 1930 Ford Model A hot rod to the 'River Bottom' which lies between Cameron and Cameron Mills and the place where I once camped as a kid. "River bottom" is a very old local term and the reference is unique to this part of the country and simply means a flat area in the valley with a river running through it. In the years before flood control dams were built in the 1950's and '60's, this valley area flooded every spring depositing rich top soil as the river receded. It was pretty much the same yearly cycle the farmers in Egypt experienced 3,000 years ago when the Nile flooded. As a farmer, if you owned a part of the 'river bottom' as your farm acreage, you had very rich soil and could count on high yield crops. You could do more than survive as a farmer; you could make a profit. If you were a farmer like Uncle George up from the valley and in the high hills, your soil was usually very rocky and poor. This was as a result of the last ice age 10-13,000 years ago when the glaciers' terminal moraines left deposits of sand, gravel, and rocks after skimming off most of the rich loom and top soil and carrying it to the valleys.

On my drive there from Bath, up old County Route 10, I stayed on the narrow macadam road which is now marked 10A and passed where Erma and George's old farm house once stood. The road hasn't changed much and it still has a very high crown and feeling is the same in the car when you try drive on it. You have to really control the steering. It is no wider than it was 60 years ago, but it is far less traveled. The newer Route 10 highway has replaced it and it follows closely the route of the old dirt road that runs directly over the hill in a straighter line which bypasses the old farm. It was on this road (when it was just a dirt road) on which I drove the '39 Willys to its top speed of 60 miles per hour when it was loaded with very precious cargo. One can still see, while driving on the new road, a trace of where the old dirt road ran with a few of the remaining trees that at one time lined its banks. The new road runs a truer and straighter course parallel to where the old stage coach road originally had been built.

Driving past George and Erma's old farm, the majestic trees that stood in the front yard were still there and are as beautiful as ever. The original house, barn, and milk house have been gone for decades but the pond and side hills still look the same, albeit overgrown. A very strange and somewhat poignant feeling came over me. As I drove slowly by where the old white clap board Greek revival style farmhouse stood, I thought I could hear children's laughter. Just a bit further down the road I passed the fields I had worked as a youngster. These were the same fields that I had mowed and raked while on the seat of the orange Allis-Chambers model C tractor. A warmhearted feeling came over me as the memories came flooding back. In my mind's eye I could see Uncle George standing in the hay loft of the barn watching me operating the tractor in the field that I was now passing. I know he was watching me ever so closely to see if I was handling the tractor in a safe manner.

I drove up the dirt road to the old cemetery. It appeared as if nothing had changed over many decades. It was under these stately oaks and maples that on a hot summer day that I would stop and have my lunch and drink a quart of Kool-Aid that Aunt Erma had made for me that morning before I went off to mow the adjunct hay field. I stopped, got out, and walked down the hill and into the grave yard. I remembered that this was the same spot where Aunt Erma, Dale and I had a lunch under the trees after picking wild strawberries in the field next to it. I felt the cool air. In my mind I was once again sitting there eating a P&J sandwich and drinking sweet Kool-Aid after mowing hay.

I walked further down the hill to visit the graves of Aunt Erma and Uncle George, and their children, Dale and Thais. These are their final resting places. As a kid, I would never have contemplated that I would see their tombstones here. I am sure there will be other head stones from

George and Erma's family here in the future. There is something to be said about coming home regardless of the old saying, "You can never go home." I read the inscriptions on the head stones again, ran my fingers over the dates as my eyes moistened. I sat down on the ground and for a long time and was lost in warm thoughts and memories of the past. These four graves are the only new ones in this cemetery in almost a hundred years. The earliest graves date back to the homesteaders and farmers who were born in the 1700's and who died on their farms and were buried here, near to their land. Farmers love their land and never want to leave it. Sometimes wars interrupt plans, dreams and desires. Uncle George and all the folks buried here knew that so well. They did go home and are close to the farm and the land they once loved so much.

Driving down old Route 10 to the river bottom in the valley after leaving the cemetery, I noticed that modern progress and change somehow had missed the small towns that were struggling just to stay alive and exist. Small country stores were closed or had disappeared completely. Churches, Masonic halls, and homes were there, but sorely in need of attention. Perhaps it is not so much attention that is needed as much as a few extra dollars that budgets simply do not allow. I passed the Church where Dale and I had attended Vacation Bible School as kids and I noticed a banner was hanging on the sign in the front announcing Vacation Bible School dates for this year! Some things never change even with the passage of time. Further up the hard top road that runs along the river, I crossed the intersection where a dirt road ended. It was at this very intersection where the two wild boys, their sister and I had crossed on our way to camp over night at the river bottom decades before. I look forward to my next road trip on old County Route 10. Time has a way of playing funny tricks in your mind. In an instant I was a kid once again…

Author's Notes

A Few of the Things My Children Taught Me

Comedian Phyllis Diller always made me smile. Charlotte and I sometimes chat about old age and nursing homes and how we want a shower or bath every day and to be able sleep together at night in the same bed. Then we look at each other and laugh and say "that's not going to happen and if that's what we want we better take care of it ourselves because the kids aren't going to help us." We may have subconsciously picked this idea up from Phyllis Diller as she said so many times in her act, "Always be nice to your children because they are the ones who will choose your rest home."

Rest homes or not, our children have taught me many things that will carry me well into old age with fond memories and miles of smiles. Our eldest daughter Tonja, taught me that as a three, four and five year old, that she could run faster than any of the boys in our apartment complex. That it's OK to eat a worm from the flower garden and you can ride your tricycle and carry a hammer at the same time. That dirty glasses don't bother you at all even though you must wear them all the time. Amazingly, she taught me that you can walk, even with both your feet and legs in a brace after sleeping in it all night and do it with a smile. And the biggest smile of all was at Christmas when Santa brought her a poodle puppy. Oh, how she loved that puppy but was willing to share her with the rest of the family. She taught me that sharing is a gift. She taught me patience and how to forgive. She taught me what it means to be a friend and how friends are friends forever and are not forgotten. She taught me the love a daughter has for her Dad and her Mom. Tonja demonstrated how to be a loving wife to Matt and wonderful Mother to Kyle and Daniel.

154

Our second eldest, Tammy, also taught me about her love for Dad and Mom in her own special way She demonstrated her love of animals including: gerbils, kittens, puppies, hamsters, an aquatic newt, ducklings, frogs, toads, and every living thing that crossed her path. She demonstrated her love of teaching and of art and having students develop their talents and strengths to the best of their abilities. Tammy as a Scout Troop leader encouraged young boys and taught them the 'art' of how to grow into manhood. She modeled what a Scout is and what Scouting is by camping out with them year 'round. As a single Mom, she raised Gavin, nurtured him, guided him, loved him, and, yes, ran a tight ship and knew when and how to discipline him.

Tammy taught me how to be a free spirit when she appeared at the front door one summer day as a little girl in just her underwear with her sun suit in hand because, "It's too hot outside." She loved Grandma's oil paintings and showed us how to "Fix them" when she climbed up on the sofa with crayons in hand to add more color to them. She brought 'color' into my life.

Our son Todd showed me the devoted love a Father has for his daughter, Hanna. He demonstrated his love everyday they were together. His patience was endless. Todd amazed me with his understanding of Dungeons and Dragons, *Star Wars* and his Star Wars collection. His love and skill both as a fisherman and hunter still boggles my mind as he has insight and skill far beyond what I could ever wish to accomplish. He has a love of the outdoors and an independent spirit.

Todd has strength of character and perseverance to overcome adversity. His commitment first to finish his Associate's degree and then sacrifice and commit to earning his Bachelor's degree at middle age and working while attending Alfred demonstrates his values as a person. I am so proud to have him as our son.

I love all three of you equally and for whom you are individually. Thank you for the gift of love and everything you have given me individually and collectively.

Gary J. Buehler, Ph.D.

ACADEMIC BACKGROUND

1986-1989   Ph.D.,Union Inst_tute and University, OH.
Dissertation Title: *Change, A Case Study of Implementing The Effective School; Model in A K-12 District.*

1977-1978   C.A.S. in Educational Administration, State University of New York, Brcckport.

1975-1977   M.S. in Educatioral Administration, State University of New York, Brcckport.

1961-1966   B.S. in Comprehensive Science, Roberts Wesleyan College, N. Chili, New York.

UNIVERSITY EXPERIENCE

1990-1997   Adjunct Professor at St. Lawrence University, NY, Department of Educational Administration, Graduate School.
        EDAD 5=2 The Negotiation Process
        EDAD 5=7 School Law

1990-2005   Adjunct Professor for Learners and as a Member of their Ph.D. Committee for The Union Institute and University, OH. Currently working with several Ph.D. Candidates.

1999-2001   Adjunct Professor for State University of New York, Oswego and the Central New York BOCES District Superintendents.
Superintendent Development Program

| 2001-2005 | Visiting Full-time Assistant Professor Position, at State University of New York, Oswego, School of Education, Department of Curriculum and Instruction, Graduate School. |

> EDU 502 Models of Education
> EDU 548 Reflective Teaching Methods.
> EDU 594 Integrated Methods
> EDU 200 Critical Thinking about Home, School, and Community

| 2005-2013 | First Core, Second Core, and Mentor Faculty member at The Union Institute and University, Ohio. |

ADMINISTRATIVE EXPERIENCE

| 1997-2001 | Superintendent of Schools of the Oswego City School District, Oswego, New York. Retired June 30, 2001 after 35 years in public education and 20 years as a Superintendent of Schools. |

| 1989-1997 | Superintendent of Schools of the Gouverneur Central School District, Gouverneur, New York. |

| 1984-1989 | Superintendent of Schools of the Williamson Central School District, Williamson, New York. |

| 1981-1984 | Superintendent of Schools of the Parishville-Hopkinton Central School District, Parishville, New York. |

| 1980-1981 | High School Principal, Parishville-Hopkinton Central School District, Parishville, New York. |

| 1979-1980 | Director of Magnet School Curriculum and Development, Rochester City School District |

1978-1979	Director of Science K-12. Rochester City School District, Rochester, New York.
1977-1978	Director of Elementary and Secondary Education Act K-12, Rochester City School District, Rochester, NY.
1975-1976	Project Director for Unified Science 9-12, Rochester City School District, Rochester, New York.
1968-1974	Evening Adult Education and GED Programs. Rochester City School District

TEACHING EXPERIENCE

1975-1978	Edison Technical High School. Chemistry, Earth Science, General Science. Rochester City School District
1971-1975	Interim Junior High. Learner-Centered School. Rochester City School District. Science Teacher.
1966-1971	Jefferson High School. Chemistry, Earth Science, General Science. Rochester City School District.

CREDENTIALS

School District Administrator, Permanent, New York State.

School Administrator and Supervisor, Permanent, New York State.

Teaching Certificates, Permanent, New York State
in Biology, General Science, and Earth Science.

EXPERIENCE AND EXPERTISE

* Learner-Centered Schools and Teaching
* Impact of Power Deregulation
* Nuclear Power Revenue Stream
* Alternative School Planning and Implementation
* Administrator and Teacher Evaluation
* Labor Negotiations (Win-Win Negotiations)
* Labor-Management Committee Implementation and
      Functioning
* Authentic Assessment
* Cooperative Learning
* Flexible Scheduling (Semestering)
* Integration of Curriculum
* Learning/Teaching Styles
* Multi-Age Grouping
* Portfolios
* Shared Decision Making and Teaming
* Team Building and Consensus
* Change Theory
* Teacher Evaluation Rubrics
* School Law
* Employee Disciplinary Hearings (3020-a and Section 75)
* Student Disciplinary Hearings and Due Process
* SAVE Legislation and Application
* Models for Teaching
 * The Reflective Process
* Hearing Officer for PL 94-142

BOARD OF DIRECTOR POSITIONS HELD

* Arts and Culture for Oswego County
* Greater Oswego Chamber of Commerce
* Steering Committee for Team Sheldon
* Steering Committee for Family Services for Oswego County
* Cooperative Organization for Public Education (COPE)
* United Way of Greater Oswego County, Inc.

* Gouverneur Foundation, Inc.
* North Country Study Council
* St. Lawrence Valley Chapter of the Boy Scouts of America
      (President)
* International Chapter of Phi Delta Kappa (President)
* The Union Institute and University Graduate Alumni/ae
      Board (President)
* Pultneyville Historical Society (President)
* RSR (President)
* Life Performance Institute

PRESENTATIONS, WORKSHOPS, AND CONSULTANT WORK

* National Center for Effective Schools
* State Education Department, Effective Schools
* State Education Department, Excellence and Accountability
* New York State School Boards Association, Roles of Board
      and Superintendent
* Foundation for Curriculum Development, the Netherlands
* Three Year School Exchange Program in St. Petersburg,
      Russia
* New York State United Teachers, Shared Decision Making
* New York State Parent-Teachers Association, Shared
      Decision Making
* National Conference on School Restructuring
* Association for Supervision and Curriculum Development on
      Restructuring
* Eastern Michigan University, Training on Empowerment
* Ann Arbor School District, Site Based Management
* New Hampshire State Education Department,
      Superintendent Training
* Northeast Effective Schools Consortium
* Mid-Hudson Administrative Training Center, Effective
      Schools
* Monroe 2 BOCES Training in ESP Science Education
* Xerox Science Consultant Programs
* American Chemical Symposiums

* Science Teachers of New York State
* Kodak Council of Scientific Societies
* Rochester Industrial Management Council
* New York State Education Department on In-service
        Education
* St. Lawrence-Lewis BOCES on the Role of the Board of
        Education
* Jefferson-Lewis BOCES on the Role of the Board of
        Education
* Phi Delta Kappa Training on Educational Initiatives
* North Rose-Wolcott Board of Education, fall of 2005.
        Design, administer, and summarize a survey for all
        Board members and District Administrators. Design
        and lead a workshop on identifying and establishing
        performance goals for 2005-06.

PAPERS AND PUBLICATIONS

Buehler, Gary J. "Unified Science Education for Rochester".
        The Science Teacher Bulletin. Vol. XLIV. No. 2 and Vol. KLV
        No. 1 1980-1981
Buehler, Gary J. "Liberty Makes Cents to North Country Students".
        NYSSBA Journal. August 1983
Buehler, Gary J. and Hentcey, Kathleen.
        "A Wilderness Experience — Parishville —
        Hopkinton Students Learn Survival". *NYSSBA Journal.* August
        1984
Buehler, Gary J. and Brown, Jane.
        "Employee Recognition The Morale Booster".
        NYSSBA Journal. January, 1995
Buehler, Gary J. "A Curriculum Development Planning Model That
        Works". *The Council Journal.* Vol. 5, No. 2. May 1986
Buehler, Gary J.; Stieglbauer, Suzanne; Turner, Mark.
        "Facilitating Process: Integrating CBAM Approaches Into
        Implementing an Effective Schools Model".
        The Council Journal. Vol. 7, No 1, January 1989

Buehler, Gary J. and Battaglia, Michael.
    "Does The School Board Really Control Taxes?"
    NYSSBA Journal. March 1990

Buehler, Gary J. "Characteristics and Considerations for Change and
    Restructuring". Presented at the Annual Commissioner's
    Conference for School Administrators and the New Hampshire
    School Administrators Association. June 25, 1990

Buehler, Gary J. and Mesibov, Donald.
    "Shared Decision Making: The Route To
    Restructuring and Shared Decision Making". NYSUT-AFT
    Educational Conference. November 16, 1990

Buehler, Gary J. and Mesibov, Donald.
    "Shared Decision Making As The Route To
    Restructuring Our Schools". Tenth Annual Statewide
    Conference on In-service Education. December 2-4, 1990

Buehler, Gary J. and Holena, Lauren.
    "Elementary Principals: Caught Between A Rock
    And A Hard Place". Skidmore College. March 4, 1990

Buehler, Gary J.
    "Shared Decision Making: Friend or Foe?" *Education News*.
    Vol 4, No 19. October 28, 1991

Buehler, Gary J.; Berry, James; Small, Mary Margaret.
    "Characteristics and Considerations for Change".
    The Council Journal. Vol 8. No 1. May 1991

Buehler, Gary J.; Battaglia, Michael; French, Lauren.
    "Fantastic Theatrics of the Superintendency".
    The School Administrator. Vol 49, No 2. February 1992

Buehler, Gary J. and Mesibov, Donald.
    "Shared Decision Making: The Route to Restructuring for
    Instructional Improvement". *The Council Journal*. Vol 11,
    No 1. April, 1994

Buehler, Gary J. and Berry, James.
    "Restructuring School Governance through Shared
    Decision Making". *The Council Journal*.
    Vol 11, No 1. April 1994.

Buehler, Gary J.
>"Structural Participation from the Superintendent's Perspective". Possibilities Catalog: The Quest for Equity in Education. The University of the State of New York, State Education Department. May 1994

Buehler, Gary J.; Berry, James; Tracy, Jackynn; Morre, Duane H.
>"Site-Based Decision Making". Secondary Education Today. *Journal of MASSP*. Vol 35, No 4. Spring 1994

Buehler, Gary J. and Cook, Roger B.
>"Dear Teachers.....Here's What We Told Our Teachers We Expect of Them". *The American School Board Journal*. Vol 183, No 8. August 1996

Buehler, Gary J. "Sheldon Round Table"
>Leadership for Oswego County. 1999

Buehler, Gary J. "The Superintendent's Corner".
>Weekly Column in the *Daily Palladium Times*. !997-2001

Buehler, Gary J. "1999 Progress Issue".
>*Oswego County Business Magazine*. January 1999

Buehler, Gary J. "Spotlight on a Retired Superintendent: How My Journey Led to My Baker's Dozen" *Sheldon's Sphere*. Vol. 9: Issue 1, spring 2002

RECENT HONORS AND AWARDS

1999 Nominee for New York State and National Superintendent
of the Year

1997 Kappan of the Year awarded by the International
Chapter of Phi Delta Kappa(ADK)

1997, 1998, 1999, and 2000
National What Parents Want in Their Schools Award

PERSONAL

Blessed with excellent health and humor. Life is good! Married since 1960 to Charlotte Kathryn Morris, a practicing psychologist. Three children, son Todd and daughters Tonja and Tammy.

Four grandchildren, Kyle, Daniel, Hanna, and Gavin.

Other enjoyments include: travel both to Europe and around United States with Charlotte, metal sculpting, wine making, reading/research, target shooting, photography, brewing gourmet vinegars, poker, designing and building hot rods and, most important, time with our grandchildren.

At the current time, I am exhibiting many pieces of art and metal sculptures at the Artisans' Loft at The Landing at Pultneyville, NY and finishing the construction of a 1932 Ford hot rod.

Family Photos

Framed photo of Joseph Jensen
that sits on my dresser

Joseph Jensen in framed photo
that sits on my dresser.

My mother Emma Buehler and
my grandmother/mother Helen Buehler.

Fred Buehler grandfather/father as a younger man.

(Date unknown)

Grandmother, mother, great-grandmother,

and baby Gary at Carl and Johanna Rightmire's farm

in Pennsylvania, August 1940.

August 8th, 1942, Gary's birthday

(Two years before contracting polio)

Gary and grandparents Fred and Helen Buehler

October 1943 (before adoption)

Uncle/brother Paul and Gary

Home from hospital after polio on the

front lawn of 1519 Emerson Street

Wedding day for Uncle Fritz and

Aunt Emma Buehler

Eugene Buehler (date unknown)

Wedding day for Aunt Erma and Uncle George Spears

Original farmhouse and barn, circa 1947

Aunt Erma and Uncle George Spears, circa 1947

Growing family: (front) Helen and Lorna

(back) Renee, George, Erma, and Dale

Helen and Dale Spears on new bikes won by

selling the most newspaper subscriptions

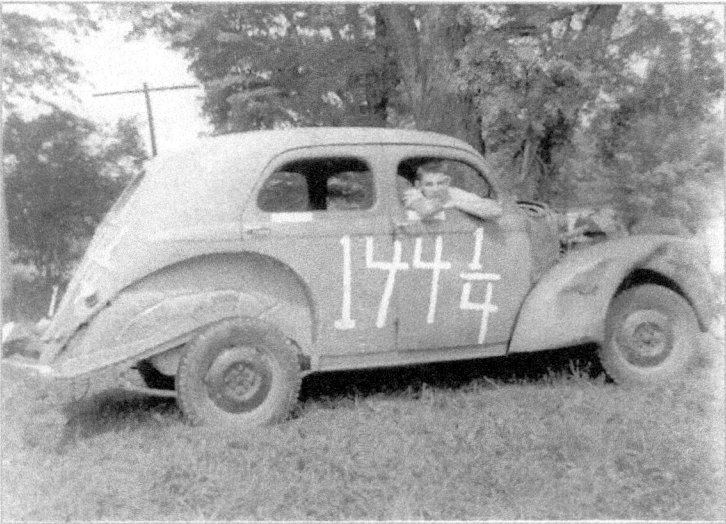

Earl and the Willys

Willys Race Day

The Circus Comes to Town

Return of the Circus

(center) Helen with sisters Lorna and Thais

Allis

The Little AC Tractor

(Helen, Lorna, Renee, Dale, and Thais)

Damn Fools

George Horeth, left; Gary, right

Our Wedding. July 30th, 1960

Lorna Spears, Pam Meyers, Kay (Charlotte), Gary,

Paul Buehler (uncle/brother), Larry (Paul's son)

www.ingramcontent.com/pod-product-compliance
Lightning Source LLC
La Vergne TN
LVHW011419080426
835512LV00005B/144